ACCULTURATION AND DOMINATION IN TRADITIONAL ASIAN MEDICAL SYSTEMS

BEITRÄGE ZUR SÜDASIENFORSCHUNG
SÜDASIEN-INSTITUT
UNIVERSITÄT HEIDELBERG

BAND 160

FRANZ STEINER VERLAG
STUTTGART
1994

ACCULTURATION AND DOMINATION IN TRADITIONAL ASIAN MEDICAL SYSTEMS

edited by

DOROTHEA SICH

and

WALTRAUD GOTTSCHALK

FRANZ STEINER VERLAG
STUTTGART
1994

Die Deutsche Bibliothek – CIP-Einheitsaufnahme

Acculturation and domination in traditional Asian medical systems / ed. by Dorothea Sich and Waltraud Gottschalk. - Stuttgart : Steiner, 1994
(Beiträge zur Südasienforschung ; Bd. 160)
ISBN 3-515-06556-3
NE : Sich, Dorothea [Hrsg.]; GT

Herstellung: Strauss Offsetdruck GmbH, 69509 Mörlenbach,
Printed in Germany

Contents

Preface

The Third International Congress on Traditional Asian Medicine (ICTAM III) 1990 in Bombay was an opportunity for a German sponsored group of twelve anthropologists and physicians to present a Symposium on Acculturation and Domination in Asian Medical Systems. This symposium was organized to point to a shortcoming and at the same time to a great challenge within cultural medical anthropology, namely understanding health care as a functional element of a cultural system, akin to language, religion and kinship. These are systematically studied by anthropologists as functional systems of culture. The ICTAM symposium was organized on the premise, that health care should be studied similarly as a functional system of culture, as it structures experience and practice of individuals and groups in their efforts to cope with problems of sickness within their cultural sphere of action. The contributors were selected on the basis of extensive experience in studying aspects of health care in various Asian social and geographical settings. Seven of the twelve presentations, partly in an adapted form, are published now in this reader. The papers, although very different in content illustrate the problems, the shortcomings and the challenges. Thanks to the graciousness of the South Asia Institute, this publication has finally become possible and can be available to a broader audience.

Dorothea Sich — Institute of Tropical Hygiene and Public Health
Waltraud Gottschalk — South Asia Institute
January 1994 — Heidelberg University

Introduction

Dorothea Sich

Medical systems influence each other everywhere and have always done so. Nevertheless acculturation and domination in medical systems have become a problem for present health care efforts, especially in so-called developing countries. Medical anthropology is challenged to provide tools for the better understanding of problems arising due to changes in existing health care systems. Health care systems should be considered as cultural systems of meaning embedded into the cosmology of cultural groups, akin to language, religion and kinship. These should be systematically studied by anthropologists as functional systems of culture. As such they structure experience and practice of individuals and groups in their efforts to cope with problems of sickness within their cultural sphere of action.

Developments in medical anthropology (especially in the American branch) have indicated that examining cultural patterns of metaphor and meaning may become a promising key to a better understanding of developments in health care. Observations in the field demonstrate that it has become imperative to extend transcultural health care research beyond a mere biomedical understanding of cultural development and change in health care. Modern placebo research has given some indication of the power of cultural metaphors on the biological process of healing. Modern schools of psychosomatic medicine and of physiology, using paradigms of systems theory and semiotics, are coming very close to rediscovering core symbolic elements of culture as being most powerful in affecting human biology. Medical anthropology and medicine, however, have yet to discover this profound practical impact of the metaphoric power of culture on the healing process and on health in any cultural sphere of action. If the function of health care is to integrate and deal with sickness within the cultural process, then it is obvious that biological parameters of morbidity and mortality do not suffice for an estimation of this healing power of culture. There is a need to develop ideas and eventually parameters, to evaluate and to compare this phenomenon transculturally and over time in order to estimate the impact of change on this function.

The contributions to this volume deal with observations on the cultural context of health care and the impact of "development" and change. They are published with the hope to stimulate awareness towards the ethnocentric preconceptions with which most medical and anthropological research conducted in health care, in order to estimate development and change, so far indulges only in comparing the impact of traditional healers and their drugs and techniques with those of modern healers and their methods. The cultural context of health care becomes of interest to evaluators only then, when it appears as a hinderance to effective modernization of existing systems. The cultural patterns of coping and the capacity of people to deal with sickness effectively in everyday life is not yet recognized as an important aspect of health care. These subtle cultural observations, integrative interpretations, and awareness of the ethnocentric element in any intercultural comparison as practiced by earlier anthropologists, e.g. Victor Turner and Lévi-Strauss, have by no means become the routine in medical anthropology that they should be today.

Lévi-Strauss, in analysing a shaman's healing activity, has identified three powers which are effective in the cultural process of healing. The shaman's healing capacity is demonstrated to be just one of these in the process to restore health. Of equal importance is the client's faith in his capacity to heal. And the third essential element is the supporting conviction within the community that "it will work". If any of these three components in the process is lacking in strength, the result may well be failure. We, however, have made little effort in trying to understand how the third power, that of the supporting conviction has a bearing on health and healing together with the other two powers. To study only the shaman and his client or the specialist and his patient doesn't suffice to understand health care and to estimate its quality. The role that cultural ecology, represented by the supporting group, plays in this interaction, is of equal importance. These three elements should be considered together as important in producing health within a cultural system of meaning.

Studying cultural systems of health care is being regarded as obsolete by some cultural anthropologists, because they are supposedly vanishing. They do not simply vanish, of course. They may be destabilized and in consequence disintegrate. If we conceive medical care as a cultural system of meaning, it becomes obvious that specific and meaningful cultural patterns enable individuals and groups to deal with sickness as a process requiring mutual effort, individually and socially .

The western natural science paradigm of health works reasonably well in the "Lebenswelt" within its own sphere of origin. It does not present universal values and truths in the cultural sense. The structure of the cultural patterns of meaning concerning health, illness and medicine in the "Lebenswelt" of people in different cultural settings correspond powerfully with respectively different patterns of behaviour. Ignorance of this fact has resulted in the failure of many health development projects. But of even greater concern should be the effect of 'development' and change on cultural patterns of health care within these settings as it affects the systems of meaning for behaviour. Wherever traditional systems of meaning and their respective systems of behaviour are forced to absorb too many new elements these systems are destabilized and disintegrative with the consequence of impaired coping capacity, impaired capacity to deal with sickness efficiently in every day life and within the cultural process. In any given cultural ecology under high pressure to absorb new patterns of health care, a confusion eventually arises which is caused by mixed traditional and modern concepts that cannot be integrated meaningfully. This may impair participants in their capacity to cope with sickness and even the communication efforts of modern health personnel.

"Health" is a problematic concept especially as it is used in development practice. Here it reflects the cultural reductionist structure of "modern" health sciences. In this context it functions as a universal value. Nevertheless it does not reflect the multiplicity of cultural constructions of health. This "modern" concept of health depends on the western paradigm of biomedicine. In consequence present health care development is promoted on the basis of a cultural reductionist concept of health, which has become a universal political value. Anthropologists as well as physicians are confronted and challenged with acculturation and domination already on the conceptual level. The papers collected for an interdisciplinary symposium presented investigations into problems of acculturation and domination in Asian medical systems. It was possible to include the paradigmatic problems into the discussion of presented field data. The symposium thus became a platform and starting point for further creative and productive exchange about the observed complex problems in this sphere.

In this volume we have collated examples and analyses of acculturation and domination processes in specific cultural systems of health care. They shed light on the differences in accompanying problems and on the similarity of the underlying causes. The impact of medical care of the western type prevails in Asian countries as well as elsewhere. It has been introduced with an eurocentristic and universalistic attitude. "Modern" health care has remained negligent until today of traditional ways to view life and patterns of coping with afflictions including birth, illness, dying and death. In attempts to "improve" upon traditional health care and to eradicate "unhealthy" behaviour, modern health workers systematically devaluated prevailing patterns of coping, and thus began the long process of domination and acculturation in medical systems.

The contributions bring this into view in different Asian countries: Indonesia, the Philippines, Nepal, Ladakh, Fiji, Samoa and Tonga. Western medical concepts and their cultural biases were transferred to these cultures for almost one century and without reservations. They were introduced and received as signs of progress. Now it can be demonstrated how these have become an additional health burden for people in the respective countries. On the closer view, as presented in these papers, it becomes possible to grasp the socio-cultural as well as the economical aftermath. It is a hard thing, and necessary, to look at these results and to contemplate and introduce possible alternatives for improvement.

Annemiek Richters' paper is an exemplification and discussion of such results in the context of a specific case. In her study on mental health in Indonesia she points to afflictions, from which primarily women suffer. Cultural constructs of health and disease determine how coping with these afflictions in everyday life occurs. It is demonstrated how these traditional views demand careful research, ethnographic analysis and interpretation in order to understand the traditional process of coping. Simultaneously it becomes apparent how this process is afflicted by change.

Norbert Kohnen shows how western concepts of medicine are filled by people in the Philippines with meanings of their own. Health education campaigns, conducted a decade ago in a cultural reductionist manner have resulted in confused patterns of knowledge and behaviour. Modern health personnel is not any more able to communicate effectively with patients who hold these confused concepts.

Christine Loytved's research follows up on the process and results in the case of unreflected adoption of so-called traditional institutions into modern health care as practiced by WHO on "traditional birth attendants" in the South Pacific. She demonstrates the negative results of this form of forced acculturation on the traditional midwives as well as on their clients. Fruitful cooperation between traditional healing-professionals and modern health professionals may well be possible under certain conditions. This entails no attitude of superiority on the side of modern health personnel and the fostering of self-reflexive growth of the traditional professionals with their changing conditions.

Martin Gaenszle in his study on the Mewahang Rai in Nepal presents a different example of cultural communication problems and their causes. He demonstrates how traditional views on world, man and life into which medicine belongs, are only part of the problem. Another part is played by political relations of dominance and dependency. Modern health workers, on whom the communication depends in the actual case, are often part of the dominating political structure. Economical factors as well as inner-ethnical prejudices and reservations, and other causes which underlie mutual misconceptions, impair communication or make them altogether impossible. Proper analysis of such conditions can demonstrate feasibilities and limitations for meaningful integration of modern and traditional systems of health care.

Alice Kuhn has observed such growth of traditional professionals and their (partly systematic) institutionalization in the pluralistic medical system of Ladakh. She also observed, how modern health care became eventually systematically enforced through the influence of the Indian government, and how this resulted in a situation of extreme competition between different forms of medicine which coexisted peacefully before.

Ludger Albers, on the background of substantial experience with the study of culture-bound syndromes of medical anthropology and with functional syndromes of psychosomatic medicine, deals with the question of reality as a method to approach more effectively the impact of change on cultural systems of health care. Reflective and critical thinking about not only traditional systems of health care but also of the modern, is the precondition to understand and cope with our responsibility that "modern" cultural domination entails in any cultural realm, including our own.

Eduard Bonsel bears this further out. Reflective and critical thinking is desperately needed but it is hard to face the facts. A change of attitude towards these issues is essential. And that, he argues, must begin in our own minds. This is the presupposition that eventually all involved people and institutions may come to terms with the emergent situation of world wide culturally defunct health care systems.

Systematic research on acculturation and domination in medical systems is mandatory. The contributions to this volume underline this assertion. This reader is now published with the hope to serve as a stimulant for concerned people and institutions to promote, foster, develop and undertake such research.

Linkages between modernization and women's health in South East Asia: Impacts of development in Indonesia

Annemiek Richters

1. Introduction: modernization and its relation to health and disease

The modern world can be conceived of as a cloth of many colours woven from threads of capitalist (patriarchal) modes of production and distribution, and their underlying ideologies. In much of the world the magic of science, technology and so-called development seem to have won the day. Accomplishment of the technologically possible, rather than the ethically valuable, dominates aspirations. Technicians are at a premium with affect dismissed as a 'commodity' of little value during development planning-, and policy evaluation processes. Daedalus' creations lead a life of their own while we, like giddy Icarus, unmindful of warnings, allow ourselves to be carried away, careening ever onwards, bent on 'progress' and 'modernization', agents of destruction, laying waste to our natural environment, our fellow men, and ultimately, there is every reason to believe, ourselves as well.

Modernization, in addition to positive consequences for our well-being, has also precipitated a wide range of dis-eases. Ill health, for example, deriving from the struggle to survive in urban slums, from dislocation and from further stresses brought about by the destruction of traditional certainties which accompanies modernization. In the Jakarta Post of December 6, 1986, for instance, it was reported that in the last five years the number of people suffering from mental disorders in Jakarta had increased: "most of the patients are people from outside the city who came to Jakarta to find jobs. The other are State employees and poor people. These homeless live in an unhealthy environment. The depression that ensues is the earliest phase of the mental disorder."

It is now widely accepted that socio-cultural transformation affects patterns of disease in various groups. These patterns are undoubtedly significantly related to cultural sets of normative beliefs and behaviour. Hypothesizing that lifestyle - or culturally influenced behaviour - is a major determinant of community health, Sinnett and Whyte (1978) contrasted lifestyles in a rural subsistence community (in Papua New Guinea) with lifestyles in an urbanized society (Australia). The authors compared the communities with regard to such features as physical environment, social situation, human relationships and parameters of health and patterns of disease. Members of the Papua New Guinea's community, seen as self-reliant, and socially cohesive, were adjudged to be well adapted to their physical and social environment. They were free from major degenerative cardiovascular diseases and manifested little overt psychiatric illness, but suffered from both a heavy burden of infectious disease and marginal nutritional status. On the other hand, the highly industrialized Australian community was found to lack social cohesion, to depend heavily on technologies of production, and to discourage direct relationships between its members and their physical environment. The price people paid for containment of infectious disease, diminished infant mortality and extended life expectancy would seem to be increased levels of degenerative disease and of diseases caused by psychological distress.

Numerous studies in other parts of the world have produced similar findings (1). Rates of cardiovascular diseases tend to follow a gradient of economic development or modernization, industrialized nations having the highest rates. While it is clear that social and cultural factors play a role in the etiology of these diseases, the issue still is the nature of the process by which this occurs (2). As far as mental illness is concerned, many studies have confirmed that social breakdown in communities, alcoholism and drug abuse, uprooting and forced acculturation among refugees, immigrants and migrants, unemployment, problematic work relations, stressful work conditions, are all risk factors for increased rates of mental illness (3). These risks are highest during periods of rapid modernization of traditionally oriented populations.

If these findings are valid, perhaps rates of mental disorder in a population can - like child survival rates - offer an indicator for level of modernization or development.

In its development efforts Indonesia appears to have chosen on a grand scale to strive for the reduction of child mortality rates (4) by introducing 'child survival programs', neglecting, comparatively, efforts to prevent the rise of psychopathology rates. Yet, we may wonder, what is the value of child 'survival' efforts, if we don't simultaneously guard the mental (and, of course, physical) health of the nurturers and educators of these children as well as, more broadly, the sanity of our species and the integrity of its natural environment?

These are large questions which cannot be handled within the scope of one article. I will confine myself to a greatly neglected but important area of research in development studies: the impact of modernization on the mental health of women. Specific references are made to the context South East Asia, Indonesia in particular. Since the case material I need for a clarification of my line of reasoning is scarce I will occasionally refer to case studies from other parts of the world. The purpose of this article is not to give a well-rounded presentation of a strictly defined problematic, but rather to introduce the reader to a field of study that is only in its earliest stage of development. The emphasis lies on the exploration of a methodology appropriate for the study of women's mental health crossculturally and its linkages with modernization processes.

2. A critical evaluation of modernization processes by means of the study of women's dis-eases

The study of women's mental health in the developing world not only casts doubt on the value of modernization processes for women, but also challenges scientific disciplines such as transcultural psychiatry and development studies in so far as these are specifications of the modernization paradigm. The main presupposition of this paradigm is that western development, and western science as its mediator, should serve as a model for development across the globe modernization equals westernization.

In sociopolitical theory and philosophy the view of history in which the West leads the rest of the world down the road of modernity has concomitantly come increasingly under attack. In fact worldwide resistance to this view has taken the form of a critique of those ideological and cultural forms of modernization displayed by the global hegemony of the industrialized powers. This critique is often a silenced form of critique. Some social scientists consider it, precisely for this reason, as their most important task to give voice to this critique. They work from the starting point that one way of trying to understand the impacts of modernization in people's daily lives is first to regard the global 'civilizing' process through the eyes of those who suffer most intensely under its (unintended?) negative consequences, and then to listen to their (often silenced) voices.

I will do so by focusing on women, who as a group suffer more from the negative consequences of modernization than men. But I don't want to leave it with that, and also study the coping mechanisms women develop that keeps them healthy. This shift of focus may perhaps give us some answers to the often subordinated questions of 'what keeps people well under changing circumstances' and 'how can we strengthen the conditions leading to such well-being'. Those answers might be of the utmost importance for a critical assessment of the modernization processes from which only a minority of the world's population profits and which have led to the ecological crisis on micro, and macro level in which modern man is embedded.

Western feminist analyses of women's mental diseases have taught us that these dis-eases can and should be reconceptualized as silenced forms of critique of women's life world, the socio-cultural changes women are exposed to and the psychiatric diagnostic categories they are labelled with. The problem is that these analyses generally focus on mental problems of middle class western women and exclude the study of women's mental health related to class, race, religion, ethnicity and the larger political economy context (5). This means that these analyses are only of restricted value for our purposes.

A point of departure of my analysis in this article is that mental illness is as much of an issue for political economy and ideological manipulation, as it is for biology, medicine and psychiatry. One can study psychopathologies by asking how they are collectively willed into being, how they are generated by institutions, customs and practices. The pervasiveness of science and technology in the world today has created institutions (such as medicine and psychiatry) that entail total standardization and are increasingly capable of exacting conformity and, in doing so, of advancing seemingly impregnable norms.

One result of these processes is that psychiatric diagnostic categories tend to reflect the distribution of power in society and the attempts of those in power to maintain the status quo, rather than to shed light on the plurality of forms and the depth of psychic suffering. If one chooses to do the latter, one might find a view on developments in society, including developments in psychiatry and medicine, which the powers that be wish to silence. This means that we cannot study the linkages between modernization and women's health and dis-ease without simultaneously de- and reconstructing dominant psychiatric categories. Psychiatric anthropology has tried to do the latter and is in the process of developing 'cultural sensitive' methods for diagnosing of psychic suffering. Let us have a brief look at this development and see how we can make these methods more 'gender sensitive'.

3. Culture, modernization and the diagnosis of psychopathology

Psychopathology, as broadly used in this section, refers to the kind of behaviour (also designated as mental illness or mental disorder) described as bizarre, disruptive, destructive, unusual, abnormal, malfunctional, or anti-social, and responded to accordingly.

3.1. The evolutionary perspective

Incidents of psychopathology which psychiatrists observed during the colonial period were taken as variants of the classic mental disorders described in Europe. On Java mental illness, according to the German Kraeplin (1904), showed "broadly the same clinical picture as we see in our country ... The overall similarity far outweighed the deviant features". He then proceeded to describe the Malayan *amok* phenomenon as a variant of epilepsy or alternatively, catatonia (6). True, European psychiatrists were at times puzzled about the elaborate cultural encrustations which they saw as overlying the familiar 'real illnesses', yet at other times they were also struck by the barrenness, the simplicity of the clinical picture. In 'primitive' cultures schizophrenia, for example, was seen as a poor imitation of the European original, or as Kraeplin put it, schizophrenia "in a lower stage of intellectual development". As for depression, it was believed that among non-Europeans it hardly ever occurred. Kraeplin concluded that well-marked and enduring states of depression were not found among Indonesian patients, and attempted to explain this by comparing the 'psychiatrically underdeveloped population of Java with immature European youth' (7). This kind of explanation was characteristic of his time. Depression, seen as a malady of mature and sophisticated people, was more often reported as uncommon among the indigenous inhabitants of the colonies. It was believed that the inhabitants of Africa and Asia (like English women) could never attain the intelligence of the English civilised *man*, so that they could never suffer any of the 'painful' consequences of such attainment either.

3.2. Universal versus culture-bound psychopathology

Amok, a type of abnormal behaviour that did not make sense at first sight from the perspective of western psychiatric disease classifications, has been placed under the label of 'culture-bound syndromes' by successors of Kraeplin. So-called 'culture-bound syndromes' - signalling the incipient idea of 'culture as pathology' in the non-western world, while at the same time implicitly confirming western medical nosology as culture-free and therefore value-free - provided ample scope for colonial psychiatry to distinguish itself as a separate speciality. The idea that Whites (associated with culture) suffered from 'real' (natural) mental illnesses, whereas Blacks (associated with nature) had only culture-bound psychopathology, provided yet another justification of the strangeness, the otherness of non-Europeans.

The prevailing idea in comparative psychiatry has always been that cultural factors *shape* pathology, i.e. cultural factors have *pathoplastic* rather than *pathogenic* (or causal) effects. This assumes that under the surface of cultural factors, one can identify 'real entities' which are universal - and which admit investigation with universal methods, i.e. with research instruments initially constructed in the western world for epidemiological studies among western populations.

Anthropologists on the other hand have usually regarded culture-bound syndromes as disorders unique to a specific culture, presupposing thereby the *pathogenic effect of culture (8)*. These syndromes are often described as conservative types of behaviour. There may be some enhancement of status involved in certain sets of culture-bound syndromes, but even so, the effect is characteristically conservative, i.e. the enhancement accruing to the disorder does not seriously disrupt or threaten the social structure and 'outbreaks' are on the whole easily contained by the agents of social control.

Certainly such holds true, for example, for *bebainan* as recently analyzed by the Balinese psychiatrist Suryani (1984). *Bebainan* afflicts females who are strictly confined within the *puri* (the living quarters of the king and his relatives which contain many households whose members are closely related through birth and intermarriage) between the ages of 16 and 30. It is an illness provoked by the emotional stress of confinement. From a psychiatric point of view, *bebainan* can best be considered a form of dissociative behavior. But, says Suryani, this disorder can only be understood in the context of Balinese culture, a strong statement which requires further consideration. Although *bebainan* demons may be uniquely Balinese, surely neither the *puri* confinement nor the emotional stress with which Balinese women must cope are all that dissimilar from the straightened circumstances and emotional pressures which women have had to bear in other cultures and at other times. And the psyches of women under such circumstances elsewhere might also resemble those of *bebainan* cases (9). Even so, we still could speak of culture-specific forms of distress.

Until recently not much research in this area has been done. Based on research findings available (10), we can nonetheless anticipate that any changes in Balinese culture which lead to increased voluntary goal-directed action among Balinese women will be accompanied by a decrease in *bebainan* cases. History has taught us, however (11), to accept the prospect that should *bebainan* episodes decline other female disorders arising from other kinds of stresses may well emerge.

3.3. Acculturation and 'change' in psychopathology

The assumption that cultural factors have only a pathoplastic influence on culture-bound syndromes allows these syndromes to be subsumed under western-based psychiatric categories. This notion of the relation between culture and psychopathology, however, fails to capture the dynamic character of these syndromes. If cultural rules and symbols are constructed objects to which values are attributed, then it is logical to conclude that symptoms of mental illness in a particular culture are really societal value judgements of how individ-uals should *not* behave. In addition, these value judgements do not remain static but change as cultural rules and symbols are exposed to foreign influences. Lee (1981) uses cases of *amok*, *latah* and possession hysteria in Malaysia as illustrative examples of such change. Below I provide a short account of Lee's argument, for his approach gives us a hint of how we might look at other 'changes' in psychopathology as a result of acculturation processes.

In traditional Malaysian society the loss of self-control manifest in *amok*, *latah*, and possession hysteria contravenes the Malay code of *budi bahasa*. Those in the grip of these disorders can be considered as temporarily released from normative restraints. *Budi bahasa* comprises a set of ideals concerned with the maintenance of harmonious relations among individuals. A person adept in *budi bahasa* is considered *halus* (refined) and deemed worthy of respect. *Amok* (strictly a male phenomenon) gives rise to role enhancement, *latah* and possession hysteria (mainly involving women) give rise to role reversals of assigned female positions in Malay structure. The transitory loss of self-control in all three syndromes is carefully managed so that social structure is not threatened, but rather legitimated. 'Victims' are not always treated as outcasts. Instead, although they transgress the code of *budi bahasa*, it is possible to displace all blame for their behaviour to supernatural entities, whose intervention apparently supersedes all other rules governing social decorum. In this context Lee refers to Horikoshi-Roe's study (1979) of mental illness in a Sundanese village in West-Java where she points out how tolerance of mental affliction is an expression of villagers' belief in the indeterminacy of fate. Similarly, Malay tolerance of *amok*, *latah*, and possession hysteria can be explained in terms of their belief that supernatural interference is beyond human control.

Tolerance, however, has become less immediate, less apparent under the impact of modernization. Psychiatric definitions have intruded upon traditional beliefs. While the syndromes have not become obsolete as a result of modernization, they have gradually assumed new functions which reflect changing structural conditions. To fit the syndromes into the western model of mental health and illness, they are endowed with new meanings. As such we may legitimately wonder whether they are indeed still 'the same' syndromes.

Amok, which nowadays is designated as criminal behaviour, has lost all former heroic connotations. It has become a psychiatric disease. *Latah*, on the other hand, is still considered by many Malays as an acceptable, if somewhat strange, clownish form of behaviour, one that does not require psychiatric intervention. Where possession hysteria is concerned, a form of epistemological syncretism has developed, so that some Malays combine modern and traditional explanations to account for the phenomenon. They claim that victims of possession hysteria suffer initially from emotional problems which, if unresolved, develop into the condition known as *lemah semangat* (weak soul), thus rendering them susceptible to spirit possession. This traditional explanation has been 'modernized' by the inclusion of intervening psychological states in the cause-effect theory of spirit possession.

Ong (1988) analyses in some detail the consequences of this modernization on women affected by possesssion hysteria. She describes how 'traditional' explanations of 'possession hysteria' (*kena hantu*) still exist next to 'syncretistic' and 'modern' explanations. In the latter case the term *peyakit histeria* is applied.

From Islam, Malays have inherited the belief that men are more endowed with *akal* (reason) than women, who are overly influenced by *hawa nafsu* (human lust). Women's spiritual frailty, polluting bodies, and erotic nature make them especially likely to transgress moral space, and therefore permeable by spirits. While spirit possession traditionally was mainly manifested by married women, given the particular stresses of being wives, mothers, widows, and divorcees, with urbanization and industrialization since the early 1970s it became overnight the affliction of young, unmarried women employed in modern organizations. These women's intrusion into hitherto forbidden spaces gave rise to the experiences of anxieties about awaiting punishment. While spirit imagery for female workers gave symbolic configuration to their fear and protest over social conditions in the factories, these signs were transformed by the organizations' management into an idiom of sickness. In the manager's view, 'hysteria' was a symptom of physical adjustment as the women workers 'move from home idleness to factory discipline'.

We are confronted here with a by no means uncommon biased view of the work load of rural women in Malaysia and beyond. Sources of 'stress' (*susah-payah*) for these rural women are first and foremost overwork, other sources being family difficulties, illnesses, accidents, and societal and religious pressures (Kimball & Craig 1988). From the women's point of view, it was therefore not so much physical adjustment that plagued them in the factories, but transgression of indigenous boundaries governing proper human relations and moral justice. In the discourse of the management, physical 'facts' that contributed to spirit possession were isolated, while psychological notions were used as explanation and as technique of manipulation. Both biomedical and psychological interpretations of spirit possession were used to define the affliction as an attribute of individuals rather than stemming from the general social situation. Scientific concepts, like *penyakit histeria*, pharmaceutical treatment, and behavioral interventions all identified and seperated recalcitrant workers from 'normal' ones disruptive workers became patients.

This mechanism of transformation of social, cultural and moral problems into physical problems has been extensively described in all its varieties in medical anthropological literature. Greek immigrant women factory workers in Montréal, Canada, for instance, say that they are often overcome by 'attacks' of *nevra* (nerves) which they experience as a 'boiling over' or as a 'bursting through the skin'. *Nevra* can sometimes explode into hysterial and violent rage leading to spouse and child abuse. Women say that what precipitates these attacks are worries - worries related to poverty, to work stress, to household disruptions and disorder related to the new 'double day' work schedules. Canadian physicians diagnose a 'depression' or an 'anxiety neurosis' for which they prescribe valium or another tranquillizers (Scheper-Hughes & Lock 1986). In factories in Malaysia and Montréal, and in many other places in the world, the social and macro-economic dimensions of the 'dis-ease' women suffer from are thus mystified by these transformations of complaints. Negative and hostile feelings, feelings of powerlessness and helplessness, feelings of discontent with the social environment, all potential forms of protest, are transformed into symptoms of diseases. Ong describes that even factory workers themselves start to internalize the 'western medical scientific discourse' adopted by the managers of the factories.

3.4. A reconceptualization of psychopathology

Lee's historical analysis and Ong's analysis of contemporary processes focus on change in indigenous conceptualizations of, and responses to 'abnormal behaviour' under the influence of both western psychiatric definitions and western treatment of this conduct. Of late efforts have increased to subsume indigenously recognized illnesses (folk illnesses) as culture-bound syndromes within the rubric of the most recent western psychiatric classification system: DSM-III (Diagnostic and Statistical Manual of Mental Disorders, Third Edition). How should we evaluate these efforts? First of all, we need to be aware that DSM-III is "a symbol system, one that condenses core meanings and value orientations in American society, in American psychiatry and in the current politics of the American Psychiatric Association" (Kleinman 1987:51). The use of DSM-III as a guideline for determining clinical psychiatric types in countries throughout in the world - as it has been applied on a grand scale in WHO studies - has evoked sharp criticism from anthropologists. In the context of this article the most salient objection to this practice is that the DSM-III classification by intruding ideologies about the western 'self' into other parts of the world precludes the possibility of identifying culture *specific* affective disorders and idioms of distress. A true confrontation between DSM-III - seen as a culture-bound system (of knowledge) - and other culture-bound psychiatric systems might enable us to overcome the current inertia of ethnocentrisms which afflicts modern, western internationalized psychiatry. This confrontation could help psychiatrists to break out of confining paradigms, enriched by new research findings, new perspectives and new theoretical insights (12).

Such an exchange would challenge in the first instance the cultural parochialism of western psychiatry. It might lead to transcending the prevailing contrast between the 'real psychopathology' of western man and the 'culture-bound psychopathology' of non-western peoples. It could help elucidate how *all* psychopathology results from the interplay of biological, psychological, social and cultural factors. True discussion would have to involve cultural anthropologists as well, encouraged to transgress standard disciplinary boundaries and to develop an interest in clinical questions. Such broadening of interests might allay the irritation many psychiatrists, and even anthropologists (13), now admit when confronted with the one-sidedness of anthropologial studies of mental health problems. The Indonesian psychiatrist Salan and American anthropologist Maretzki (Salan & Maretzki 1983), for example, critize Connor's anthropological presentation of mental health problems on Bali as "totally one-sided without equal consideration given to both the psychiatric and anthropological sides of this subject" (p. 407). Connor does not differentiate between mental health problems and treats all these problems as part of one sweeping category. As a result her approach of psychiatric care is one-sided and does not serve the people among whom she did her research. Addressing Indonesia's mental health services policy needs, Salan and Maretzki rightfully call for combined clinical and cultural research (14).

4. Modernization and women's mental health in Indonesia

4.1. Housewifization as a concomitant of modernization

Many researchers have argued that an emphasis on promoting women's health directly affects the overall improvement of health in the Third World. To be sure, where women function as family health providers and promoters, food producers and preparers, water carriers, etc. any temporary breakdown in their health may immobilize the entire day-to-day well-being of their families. Traditionally women have often been instrumental in the health maintenance of their society. Owing to various articulations of modernization in Third World countries, however, including urbanization, industrialization, mechanization, medicalization, cash-crop production, and secularization, women seem to be losing influence steadily at the level of maintaining moral and symbolic order, as well as, for instance, in regulating daily health practices. There is more and more evidence accruing that many development projects which the West has launched in the 'underdeveloped' world have worked to the disadvantage of women (15). These projects have stimulated processes which erode women's traditional power over resources. They also have detrimental effects on women's health, and on the health of the family members for whom women provide and care.

Are women strong enough to cope with these various setbacks? Or do their losses affect their mental health? And if so, how? We need to consider the possibility that the stereotypical images which many western (male) development planners have of women (including ideologies that seek to exclude women from many important areas of modern life and confine them to their 'natural place', the domestic sphere), images which they introduce through their development efforts, actually reduce women from relatively independent to dependent personalities, prone to depression.

Bennholdt-Thomsen, for instance, demonstrates in her article 'Why do housewives continue to be created in the Third World too?' (1988) that the housewife model constitutes the theoretical core of most women-related development programmes and policies. To be defined as a housewife does not mean that women at any time and any place *de facto* work only in the home. What would 'home' mean anyhow in many Third World countries, Benhold-Thomsen rightly asks? A wind-screen, a hut, a pavement? It means that women have to do any work at any time and any place, not paid or poorly paid, and that this low pay is justified by the fact that they are considered to be materially dependent on a male 'breadwinner', irrespective of whether there is such a man, or whether or not he is capable of providing 'bread' for the family.

This process of housewifization is described by Grijns (1987) concerning tea-pickers in West Java. The dominant ideology that women should be first and foremost housewives and mothers is used to justify paying female tea pickers lower wages than men in equivalent jobs, despite the women's greater skill, experience, and workload. More attention is paid to the interests of the male workers, for, according to the same ideology, they are the principal bread-winners for their families.

Housewifization of women also means stealing from women their own resources, which they need for their subsistence. It destroys their social networks and in many instances deprives them of the power they used to have. In Indonesia, a long-established tradition, which permitted women to use the authority conferred on them by their mother role, to go beyond narrow domestic boundaries in order to pursue economic and political activities beneficial to their families, gradually crumbles away. The Indonesian concept of *ibu* (mother) used to offer women the opportunity to overstep domestic boundaries and wield effective power. *Ibuism* at least until recently could not be equated with the English term motherhood, because it covered a wider range or roles (Djajadiningrat-Nieuwenhuis 1987). To what extent this is still so is a question that needs further research.

From a few other studies we know that women in some of the 'non-western' cultures see themselves as the central agents in the reproduction of society and culture. While men depict their world more in terms of rights, women do this more in terms of social responsibilities and the shaping of others' action by precept and example (Strathern 1987). Today, however, in some of the cultures being studied with a focus on gender related issues, the separation of the sexes no longer refers to mutually reinforcing values. The persistence of seperate domains of action effectively denies women participation in the emerging political and economic spheres within which power and authority have come to reside. Women no longer enjoy easy access to sites from which they derive power. How this affects the self-esteem of women in developing countries we scarcely know. Although we have few answers to such questions - at least, unlike in the past, we are beginning to ask them.

4.2. Deficiencies in anthropological studies

In most anthropological studies and in discussions about development and the Third World, women have, far more often than not, been omitted as significant members of their societies beyond the contexts of reproduction, childbearing and domestic functions. Women have been perceived largely as marginal, essentially little more than breeders. They have been overlooked as the active constructors of contexts and meanings which both reflect and affect their societies.

It is only during the last decade that feminist anthropologists have started to trace how western notions about health, illness and healing and western images of women influenced anthropological studies in the past. Their attention has also been directed to anthropologists' neglect of the activities, interests and perceptions of the world of women. The woman's role in health maintenance has often been passed over in silence or trivialized. Even the ritual importance of women to the whole of society has not been fully recognized. Although by now we have some information about the negative effects of development processes on the status and role of women in different societies, and about the development-related losses women have had to cope with, we still have scarcely any information about the impact of modernization on women's mental health.

What has been studied (and continues to be a popular subject) are those illnesses which specifically symbolize woman-ness, such as spirit possesion. Emphasis in many of these studies has invariably been accorded to the symbolism of participation in ritual possession cults. As a result, although possession rituals undoubtedly do treat both symbolic-social disorders *and* physical illness, we have considerable literature that illustrates the 'symbolicity' of non-westerners, but not much that points out either their empirical recognition of personal ill health, or their technical proficiency in treating disease. Nor has much been written on the relationship between possession and individual cure. On the other hand, portraits abound of 'possessed' (female) persons who are not 'really' sick, but who apply 'mystical pressure' against their relatives, manipulators who employ possession to 'gain attention' (16). No amount of searching suffices to turn up data about the actual 'pre-possession' health status of persons 'possessed', nor about the possible curative role of 'possession' as altering state of consciousness, nor about the post-possession health of the individual who has undergone the experience.

Many authors, with little access to and perhaps a matching interest in female affairs, repeatedly present spirit possession in their reports as a legitimate way for women to voice their frustration, fears, demands, and criticisms in male-dominated societies - both patrilineal and matrilineal. Frequently, when possession rituals are enacted for a woman experiencing a 'reproductive disorder', her problem is categorized by the anthropologist observer as a 'social conflict', an intrinsic part of her living in a male-controlled society. Such male rationalization of female illness represents yet another way in which western prejudices influence our interpretation of non-western research data. Not only is women's distress depicted negatively as a complaint, a 'reproductive disorder', rather than as a positive affirmation ("I want to have children") or the expression of indignation and anger, but women are regarded as 'conflict producers' who disrupt the order of the male universe with their fantastic afflictions.

This point of view is strikingly similar to the nineteenth-century western establishment notion that a woman's reproductive organs completely controlled her life. Curiously, when reading accounts of possession cults in Africa dedicated to female health, one encounters very much the same image of the woman's body. Female anthropologists stress that these analyses, couched in negative female imagery, ignore the channeling by women of their reproductive potential into positive cultural ends. In many societies women find ritual roles related to childbirth, rearing, and nurturing and extend their role to many afflicted members of society. Women's rituals play a legitimizing role in society and are useful to societies' structures in the inculcation of attitudes and beliefs. Female ritual communities often have their own models of society, distinct from male models. In these communities women create a horizontally affective association, which crosscuts otherwise hierarchic social orders. They thereby create an alternative, essential, and basic mode of human relatedness for the entire society. Repudiation or negation of the dominant male model at the logical level must, however, not be confused with objective opposition. Women's counterpart vision of misfortune need not necessarily be associated with any actual feminist challenge to male supremacy (17).

4.3. Attention to gender differences

Encouragingly, more and more studies indicate that both the models women use to conceptualize their misfortunes and the ways in which they express such misfortune differ from those of men. Whether we should, in our anthropological interpretations, 'translate' this difference in hierarchical oppositions is a question for debate. Inequality as a theoretical and practical concern is rooted in western ideas and concepts. Anthropologists have recently shown that there are palpable differences in power relations existing between men and women in non-western societies. By exploring indigenous concepts of 'agency' they challenge in their ethnographies the way in which western observers commonly have identified individual and collective action, and the power people claim for themselves. They show that inequality is not reducible to relations of domination and subordination and that anthropology needs to develop a set of theoretical concepts less bluntly crude than 'subordination', 'exploitation', or 'oppression' (18).

Siegel (1978), for example, who studied the linkage of curing rites and domestic politics among the Atjeh of Sumatra, focused on sex-related concepts of 'agency' and expressions of power. Atjeh men believe they are entitled to tell their wives what to do. The reason they feel this way is that they consider themselves to be beings of superior rationality, a quality achieved through their religion. Recitation of prayers and chant from the Koran five times a day puts them in a state of purified rationality, one in which all their energies and desires are controlled so that they can find rational solutions to whatever difficulties might arise. While men seldom speak, women chatter continuously. Unlike men, they feel no constraint to be rational, but neither do they conceive of themselves to be irrational. Rather their speech to them has authority. Women find the source for their authorative tone, however, not in the Koran but in curing rites and dreams. Sickness is a matter of spirits entering a person. As far as these spirits stand for anything at all, they are a generalized expression of women's unfulfilled desires, and therefore, perpetually adrift. While spirits do not have bodies, they do have language, however, without a means of expression. The woman, as medium, gives voice to these spirits through the physical apparatus of her body, and thereby expresses a patient's problem, an act which leads to chathartic release.

Although a woman gains some authority by acting as a medium, Siegel in no way hints at any challenge to male authority by way of these curing rites.

Sex-related expressions of distress differ across cultures. Feld (1982) describes how among the Kaluli of New Guinea anger is an extreme expression of the posture of assertion and grief. Grief, which like anger only acquires full meaning within the context of the Kaluli's preoccupation with reciprocity, is the emotion of a person reduced by devastating loss to powerlessness and vulnerability. Whoever grieves is a figure of great pathos, someone entitled to redress. Powerful in rage, in grief men are reduced to utter helplessness, weeping in a hysterical and uncontrolled manner. Women, more subdued in their anger, are also less undone, expressively, by grief. Their weeping they convert into a form of tearful song.

Abu-Lughod (1988) describes how there is not only a difference between how Bedouin men and women express distress, but also a difference among women themselves. Women's distress at such events as divorce may be articulated in two very different forms: in seeminlgy dispassionate and casual terms, conversationally, or else in impassioned poetic protest.

4.4. The political economy of health

Cross-cultural literature on differential expression of illness symptoms along sex lines is scarce. The earliest explanations of symptomatic differences, based on obvious biological differences between the sexes, were linked to women's reproductive capacities and their hormonal make-up. Such explanation has since been disputed, however, by proponents of socio-structural and psycho-social explanations. A common assumption nowadays is that women's status and roles in the social hierarchy entails stress which manifests itself in physical and psychological disorders. In non-industrialized societies we have learned that psychological disorders, not regarded as illness states, are therefore 'somatized'. Somatization refers to the presentation of personal and social distress in an idiom of physical complaints in conjunction with a coping style of seeking medical help. Patients who somatize either recurrently present for treatment with no discernible biological abnormality but bodily complaints, or else have some discernible disease but greatly amplify their symptoms and utilize medical services frequently.

How then are we to study women's distresses? Beyond dispute, western medicine has not proven very successful at acknowledging and treating psycho-social dimensions of sickness. Its record here is yet less impressive in 'developing countries' where these dimensions attract even less recognition than in the western world. Traditional medical systems *do* recognize the healing and caring abilities of women and, in certain respects the needs of patients receive more attention than in modern health care systems. It is to these traditional medical systems that women especially turn for alleviation of their complaints, either directly or else after biomedical treatment has failed to relieve their symptoms.

In rural Mexico, for instance, the anthropologist Finkler (1985) found that biomedical personnel failed to recognize women's somatized conditions as being associated with affective disorders. Women therefore went to seek alternative treatment from Spiritualist healers. Finkler's data indicates that vulnerability factors and life events promote expression of illness in women more often than in men. Women's symptoms reflect somatized conditions that amount to existential statements of distress. In these conditions particular life events play an important etiological role. Finkler's respondents indicated a high level of contentment with their feminine roles, that is, with the roles of wives and mothers to which rural Mexican women usually aspire. Women themselves linked their illnesses to loss and to their husbands' behaviour under the influence of alcohol rather than to their marital status *per se*, or even to the cultural inferiority as women.

Finkler's study is another example of the inadequacy of western models to study the indigenous perceptions of male-female relations. Western theories, however, are helpful in studying the embeddedness of Spiritualist healing rituals in structural relationships on meso- and macro-level which influence micro-level processes. Finkler argues that although participation in these healing activities promotes well-being for individuals, the rituals tend to perpetuate a societal status quo that is in many ways adverse to the real needs of these women. Thus, the often unintended effects exerted by patient-perceived positive healing outcomes is a replication of sociostructural conditions that in themselves may be illness producing. The individual woman's initial contact with Spiritualism and her subsequent recruitment into the movement may be largely linked to biomedicine's failure to alleviate female patients' somatized sicknesses. While the movement assists individuals to recuperate from their affliction, it does not address the root causes of the suffering, which lie in the effects on local level of the worldwide expansion of capitalist production processes. In order to do so we need a methodology in which a feminist psychiatric anthropology incorporates a macro political economy approach in its methodology.

5. Culture and social structure: risk or protective factors of emotional distress? The case of the Minangkabau

Much is already known about the relation between the capitalist mode of production and emotional distress in the West. The significance of gender, however, remains less clear-cut, even though most epidemiologies report a predominance of depression among women. Furthermore, no sound cross-cultural review of this issue, has been produced up to now. This is not surprising since single-culture studies requisite for such a review are scarce.

The study of Carstairs and Kapur (1976) may give us a lead for the much needed studies. This highly innovative and methodologically culturally sound epidemiological study reported that depression in Southwestern India was more frequent among men than women. This finding may be attributable to a previously matrilineal family structure. Other studies elsewhere in India show a higher prevalence of depression among women, including a study using the instrument developed by Carstairs and Kapur.

In order to gain more insight in the epidemiology of depression along gender lines, we need studies that compare risk factors (e.g. social tensions) and protective factors (e.g. social support) in different cultures. Since hierarchical relations within the family appear to play a key role in the genesis, onset, and expressive forms of emotional distress in the West as well as elsewhere, let us have a closer look at these relations and speculate how they might function as risk and/or as protective factor of depression. The society I have chosen for this investigation is the society of the Minangkabau of West-Sumatra.

5.1. The culture and social structure of the Minangkabau

The Minangkabau of West Sumatra have attracted the attention of social scientists because of their matrilineal kinship organization and the particular way in which they respond to change. They have managed up to the present day to keep their own cultural identity, despite deep-going socio-economic changes over the last century and despite their high level of geographical mobility. Does this mean that the Minangkabau manage to escape the trend towards housewifization (a risk factor for depression among women) noticeable elsewhere in Indonesia? There is some evidence that this indeed is the case.

Naim (1985) points out that it is difficult nowadays to distinguish Minangkabau cultural traits from Indonesian elements. This is a result of conscious efforts to mold a national identity and applies to almost all aspects of life. The underlying social structure and social organization, however, remain entrenched in the matrilineal system. Especially the migration (*merantau*) of men has been instrumental in maintaining this system.

The following aspects are central of matriliny among the Minangkabau:

1. cultural and social structural centrality of the mother role
2. the practicality of a major proportion of ongoing day-to-day kin-related decisions being made within moderately sized kin groups by women exercising this matrifocal role
3. the significance and regular practice of discussion and consultation as the mode of decision-making for matters involving larger kin groups and

4. the participation of women as well as men in kin and inter-kin group affairs, with mothers active in arrangement of marriages and having significant ceremonial roles (Tanner & Thomas 1985:70-71).

On first sight one may wonder if, at a more abstract level of generalization, these four points describe a situation so very different from that which obtains, for instance, in western cultures and countries. Although I can think of much literature in support of such an opinion, I shall defer further discussion of this issue here. If there are significant differences, and personally I think there are, these will be located in how these four central aspects of matriliny become operative in the daily lives of individuals, both in the public and private domains.

In most studies about West-Sumatra one finds chapters about the *formal* authority of Minangkabau men in relation to women. These studies range from traditional accounts that report the non-existence of any such authority, to studies like the one of Tanner and Thomas which describes how, in particular cases, older in-married men can achieve some informal authority and mediating power, to personal accounts about nuclear families similar to families in Europe or North America. The relation between formal authority and informal power is, however, complicated. There is no mention in literature about the Minangkabau how informal power operates in daily life.

Postel (1985:7) suggests a few reasons for this lack. First, informal power is a part of social life that is difficult to study, since people do not easily convey much information about its intricacies and intimacies to strangers (19). Second, researchers in the past slighted the domestic sphere. Third, to see the family context as a crucial locus for the exercise of power requires a departure from a standard western view of the world. This third contention of Postel might have been true in the past, but, I feel, the women's movement has certainly changed things. Numerous studies have been published lately, moreover, on power relations between men and women and between adults and children in the home. It is there -in these accounts - we can find a number of causes (risk and protective factors) for emotional distress. But although such studies may provide us with information both of a contingent nature, responses to particular circumstances, specific biographies and the characters of the individuals involved, and of a structural nature, we should not confine our attention to the household context. Power relations at that (micro)level are related to power relations and change in power relations at the meso- and macro-levels. Studying emotional stress among individuals belonging to a certain group, both risk and protective factors can therefore provide us as well with a very important window through which to view society at large and ongoing changes which affect the emotional lives of its members.

5.2. Migration and mental health among the Minangkabau

The study of Mitchell (1969) may give us some idea of the effect of social-cultural change on the emotional lives of the Minangkabau who, more than twenty years ago, moved from the centre (*darat*) to the periphery (*rantau*). Mitchell found that in the course of one year, 10.14 % of the new cases treated in the Psychiatric Policlinic of Djakarta's Central Hospital were members of the Minangkabau ethnic group. This percentage seemed rather high since the Minangkabau comprised at the time, roughly, only 2% of Djakarta's total population. It suggested that the Minangkabau of Djakarta lived in an environment of particularly high stress and tension. Like other migrant groups, the Minangkabau had to come to terms with new value systems in an unfamiliar environment and with people who did not share with them a common tradition of social and cultural values. Besides the strong emphasis on success, traditional sanctions for failure were heavily felt. Most important still is embarrassment at returning home if a man's trip abroad has not been successful, especially if the capital for trading or the expenses for his studies had been provided collectively by his relatives. Fear of what people think of him if he has failed to realize their expectations can bring about a loss of self-respect and feelings of anxiety, which may express themselves in hypochondriases and psycho-neurotic or psycho-somatic reactions.

This process is by no means specific to the Minangkabau. In Barbados where I worked as a medical doctor in the 1970s, for instance, one could find men in the villages who suffered from what the Barbadians used to call 'the English disease'. These men had come home from England where they 'did not make it'. Ashamed of their failure they returned home and tried to hide themselves in the countryside of Barbados.

For women, according Mitchell, the results of social change were somewhat different. They deeply felt the conflict between the strict and inflexible demands of Islam and *adat* on the one hand and the relatively free and flexible norms inculcated by western education on the other. Conflict was mostly felt in the field of social relations.

Postel (1987), in her analysis of Minangkabau novels, points to another source of stress for women. Minangkabau women are traditionally associated with the centre and men with the periphery. Migration of women to the periphery means therefore a transgression of traditional boundaries. This transgression is accompanied by the inversion of the status and authority women have in the centre in the inferior position accorded to women in the periphery.

Young Minangkabau in Djakarta, then, experienced at least two decades ago extreme tension when they tried to resolve the inherent conflict between the values of the adat system inculcated since earliest childhood, and the individualistic urban culture in which they lived after their migration. Another factor which emerged from the three case histories Mitchell presents to us is that wartime conditions, the PRRI rebellion, have played an important role in the illnesses of all three patients.

In general we can say that subjectively-perceived stressful life events play a crucial role in illness when they are culturally and collectively accepted as stressful. In most instances a cognitive appraisal of one's world is primary and it is from cognitive appraisals associated with loss and disappointment that the characteristic bodily and psychological symptoms of affective disorders arise. If we take cognitive appraisals that result in depression seriously, they may be able to tell us something about what has traditionally been perceived as socially stressful. In addition they may prove revealing about the way changes in society are perceived, and the effects of indigenous perceptions of change on peoples' emotional lives. A promising place to study these micro- and macro-level disorders might be the compound of traditional healers, even though there are those prepared to argue that these healers can only handle 'traditional stresses', not tensions arising from modernization.

Such studies must be sensitive to intra-ethnic diversity, migration status, and other population characteristics. We might then achieve some needed answers to questions about the social change fomented by development processes: which are the most stressful, why and for whom in particular?

In addition to comparative studies of prevalence, illness experience and history, we need studies that compare risk factors and protective factors in different cultures. "Even quite basic questions have hardly been addressed. For example, we do not know whether marriage is a protective factor for men and a risk factor for women with respect to depressive disorders in the non-western world as it appears to be in the West. Studies of such issues, especially were they to employ ethnographic, clinical and state-of-art epidemiological methods, offer a critical opportunity to expand our parochial theories and stand at an important research frontier" (Kleinman & Good 1985:500).

Such studies might yield an answer to the question of whether matriarchy and Islam are protective factors for Minangkabau women not only as far as authority over their children and their property is concerned, but also as far as their mental well-being goes. A woman has the right to ask her husband 'to put his shoes outside the door', but does this sufficiently protect her physical well-being or solve her mental problems when, for instance, divorce is involved?

6. Conclusion

From the sixteenth century onwards, white men have been introducing diseases among populations who had no immunity against them. Epidemics of these diseases have exterminated whole societies (20). A related problem today is whether the global introduction of modernization processes and accompaning hegemonic impositions of parochial values in some form of world empire in fact threaten whole cultures with eradication. The evolutionary potential of our species to generate cultures is a contingent gift from nature to protect man against certain hazards of life. Today we have many reasons to wonder whether this precious gift has turned into a menace to nature and mankind. Has western culture lost its emancipatory potential and turned into a dominating, normalizing, constraining force worldwide? A force so strong that it has imposed itself on peoples who had no time to develop immunity against it? Or has resistance been offered right from the start, only in forms that westerners have not known how to recognize? And has a society like Indonesia been able to safeguard her feminine aspects against the influx of more masculine-oriented western value systems, which have penetrated Indonesia under the banner of modernization?

The extent to which a cosmopolitan culture has taken hold is a matter of considerable debate. To all appearance over the whole world the postcolonial period witnessed the eager embracing of both the means and goals of western modernization. This was soon followed, however, in many places by the evocation of a tragic sense of loss. Here and there by now we even encounter the massive, violent rejection of western hegemonic cultural and ideological forms. Postcolonial history has not been a simple march forwards towards 'modernity', as some social scientists would have us believe, yet, the history view that cultures have been obstinately refusing to be universalized also is inadequate: "there is around us as much intoxication with machines and gadgets as there is cultural archeology -people busy trying to revalidate once discredited traditions and revive once-forgotten symbols. There is both a submission to a dominant culture and a revolt against it" (Ajami 1981:171-172).

Accepting the fairness and validity of Ajami's claim, I would like to venture some concluding remarks about the challenge that faces (psychiatric) anthropologists who wish to study modernization and its effect on mental health.

Reviewing a number of essays in applied anthropology, Patridge and Eddy (1987) formulated the essence of applied anthropology today as "the scientific analysis of the nature of human problems amidst changing technological, environmental and social conditions. The nature of human problems is best discovered through the empirical study of the interplay between macrocosmic context and microcosmic contexts in which human beings live out their daily lives. Macrocosmic technological, economic, political and social changes today link the microcosmic units of human behavior and interactions to regional, national, and multinational organizational structures in extraordinarily complex ways" (p. 53). As part of these changing conditions we should study social-political-cultural theory and the values, assumptions, and propositions that influence and lead to policy formulation which can, as I have tried to argue in this article, adversely affect mental health. This vital area of research is not (yet) part of any serious research tradition in anthropology (Cohen 1987:146). Contemporary social science discourse is still grounded in the specific experience and interests of particular historically and geographically delimited societies, not to mention classes (21). But there are other ways of thinking and expression than those enshrined in the reified categories of dominant western epistemology.

One way to study 'revolts' against a dominant culture is to analyze mental health problems, not as expressions of individual pathology, but as (often covert) protests against all kinds of societal oppression. Most people have no access to the dominant social-cultural means of communication and interpretation. Social scientists who wish to take the plight of these people seriously will therefore have to learn their local idioms of distress. They will have to realize, for starters, that distress often presents in the form of physical symptoms. The reason for this somatization may be that it is the safest way for the people involved to call for attention, because it is the only form of expression sanctioned by dominant groups in society. We also have to appreciate that idioms of distress may differ along gender, class, and cultural lines.

If we do sincerely want to see the world through the eyes of the disadvantaged and to listen to what they have to say, it will not suffice to use western research methods and questionnaires designed by development agencies and their researchers behind their desks. To impose diagnostic systems on a worldwide basis such as DSM-III - a system that by definition excludes major forms of distress - is tantamount to the perpetuation of imperialist strategies, the indulgence of a modern form of 'cultural imperialism'. On the other hand, we should not too easily shy away from making universal claims where evidence supports such a cross-cultural assumption. Perhaps we have simultaneously to acknowledge the limitations of our western-centric conceptual apparatus and to sustain a demand for universalism while we contemplate the future meaning and debate basic normative questions. Ethically, it is urgent for us to learn to think in terms of global human interest (i.e. the sanity of our species) without ignoring all the particular needs and interests of specific peoples.

From many power practices - whether an expression of imperialistic North-South relations or as I have tried to portray in this paper gender relations - we can learn that a dominant culture at once produces and limits its own counter-cultures. Our looking at world problems and issues at the household level in 'we-they form' or 'he-she form' has precluded constructive mutual confrontation and muffled meaningful dialogue while effectively prolonging an undesirable status quo.

We have to come to terms with the full implications of what a sensitivity to other civilizations and the other gender might entail for social and political theory as we know them. One consequence might be our finally being obliged to take a good look at the (potential) rationality of affect, to study it where relevant as a (frequently muted) form of critique. In formulating social-political-cultural development theories meant to criticize and to guide policies, we should avoid reproducing the common fallacy of treating affect as a commodity. For the most part women have been the ones to suffer from this approach. Consider, for example, how pharmaceutical industries have profited by manipulating the affect of women, converting women into consumers of their products 'for their own good' (22).

Health planners commonly take as their point of departure the questions 'what makes people sick and how to cure them'? An alternative approach might be to inquire 'what keeps and/or has kept people healthy?' and 'how can we strenghten those positive forces in a changing world'? Health confirming processes may be political, economic, religious, or cultural by nature. Scientists may well consider them unscientific, magical, incomprehensible, even generally weird (Rack 1985:284). Helping identify ways to strenghten these processes, however, without succumbing to acceptance of a status quo that deprives many from participating in developing a critical awareness of the macrostructural conditions that affect their lives, is a worthy challenge which awaits the commitment of anthropologist and medical experts alike.

Notes

1. See, e.g., 'Another Development of Health'. In: *Development Dialogue.* Dag Hammerskjold Foundation, Uppsala 1978, nr. 1, pp. 1- 76.
2. See, e.g., Marmot & Syme 1976; Dressler 1984.
   See for a sample of studies about the relation between modernization and shifts in cultural aspects of psychopathology in Indonesia: Maretzki 1981. Maretzki states (p. 247) that examples must be seen as only a very incomplete and geographically biased sampling of the many interactions between Indonesian culture and mental health. Change from the formerly localised, tribal, and peasant cultures to a national and increasingly urban culture can be expected, as has been shown elsewhere, to lead to shifts in etiology, symptomatology, and other aspects of psychopathology, but there are as yet no systematic studies of the process, only the as yet undocumented impressions of practicing clinicians.
3. See, e.g., Kleinman 1988.
4. See, e.g., Sitohang n.d.. It is noteworthy that The Third International Symposium on Public Health in Asia and the Pacific Basin (Jakarta, June 6-10, 1988) focused on: "Reaching the Unreached: Leadership Development for Child Survival and Health for All".
5. Cf. e.g. Richters 1990b.
6. Emil Kraeplin (1856-1926) made his pioneer observations in transcultural psychiatry in the State Mental Hospital in Bogor (previously Buitenzorg), Java, in 1903. Boroffka commemorates the 85th anniversary of Kraeplin's visit to Buitenzorg/Bogor in a report on his own visit there in 1988. Boroffka considers Kraeplin's observations in Buitenzorg in 1903 as the starting point of transcultural psychiatry. There are other authors who share this view.

7. Cf. Maretzki 1981:240.
8. Only lately have anthropologists also undertaken the study of syndromes which they consider unique to western culture. Cf. e.g. Richters 1991.
9. Similar cases of 'spirit possession' or 'dissociative states' have been described for areas elsewhere in Indonesia, and numerous areas in other parts of the world. Djamaludin (1971), for instance, describes one such condition, hasolopan, among the Batak of North Sumatra. Hasolopan affects women more than men, and is triggered by depressive moods or frustrations. The person affected becomes possessed of a spirit (begu).
10. See, e.g., Ullrich 1987.
11. See, e.g., Showalter 1987.
12. See, e.g., Good 1987.
13. See for instance the view in this respect of the anthropologist Maretzki (1984) with regard to mental health research and mental health services in Indonesia. See for culturally oriented research developed by Indonesian psychiatrist various publications in the Indonesian psychiatric journal, Djiwa.
14. See Kleinman & Good 1985 for illustrations of the kind of research advocated by Salan and Maretzki.
15. See, e.g., Rogers 1981; Aguwa 1983.
16. See, e.g., Lewis 1971.
17. See, e.g., Hoch-Smith & Spring 1978.
18. See, e.g., Strathern 1987. In order to explain recent trends towards 'westernization', however, we should consider the legitimacy of using at least some of the concepts developed in the West to study 'inequality'.
19. See, however, Sanday (1986), who did get some information about this informal power when she studied attitudes towards rape among the Minangkabau. The Minangkabau are a relatively rape-free society.
20. See, e.g., Doyal 1979; Crosby 1986.
21. See, e.g., for a critique of this epistemology in development discourse from a woman's point of view: Kardam 1987. The books of Doan 1987 and Kua & Chye 1987 are examples of studies written for South-East Asia women, which portray the reality of women's lives nevertheless entirely from a western point of view, neglecting the validity of these writings for South-East Asian women.
22. See, e.g., McDonnell 1986.

Literature

ABU-LUGHOD, L. (1988): *Veiled Sentiments - Honor and Poetry in a Bedouin Society*. Berkeley: University of California Press.

AGUWA, M. I. ed. (1983): *Women, Health, and International Development*. Michigan State University. Proceedings of the Conference of Women, Health, and International Development. October 1982. East Lansing, Michigan.

AJAMI, F. (1981): *The Arab Predicament*. Cambridge: Cambridge University Press.

BOROFFKA, A. (1988): Emil Kraeplin and Transcultural Psychiatry - A Historical Note. *Transcultural Psychiatric Research Review* 25(3): 236-239.

BENNHOLDT-THOMSEN, V. (1988): Why do Housewives Continue to be Created in the Third World too. In: Maria MIES et al. *Women - The Last Colony*, pp. 159- 168. London: Zen Books.

CARSTAIRS, B.M. & R.L. KAPUR (1976): *The Great Universe of Kota - Stress, Change and Mental Disorder in an Indian Village.* Berkeley: University of California Press.

COHEN, R. (1987): Policy and Social Theory in Anthropology. In: E.M. EDDY & W.L. PARTRIDGE, eds. *Applied Anthropology in America*, pp. 140- 159. New York: Columbia University Press.

CONNOR, L.H. (1982): Ships of Fools and Vessels of the Divine. *Social Science & Medicine* 16: 783-794.

CROSBY, A.W. (1986): *Ecological Imperialism - The Biological Expansion of Europe,* 900 - 1900. New York: Cambridge University Press.

DJAMALUDIN, S. (1971): *Hasolopon* - A Mental Illness Occurring Among the Bataks in Tampanuli and the Karolands. *Jiwa* 4: 16-25.

DJAJADININGRAT-NIEUWENHUIS, M. (1987): Ibuism and Priyayization - Path to Power?. In: LOCHER SCHOLTEN & NIEHOF, pp. 43-52. Leiden: KITLV.

DOAN, H. (1987): *Everyday Woman: Adapting for Mid-life Change.* Petaling Java, Malaysia: Pelanduk Publ.

DOYAL, L. (1979): *The Political Economy of Health.* London: Pluto Press.

DRESSLER, W.W. (1984): Social and Cultural Influences in Cardiovascular Disease - A Review. *Transcultural Psychiatric Research Review* 21(1): 5-42.

FELD, S. (1982): *Sound and Sentiment - Birds, Weeping, Poetics and Song in Kaluli Expression*. Philadelphia: University of Pennsylvania Press.

FINKLER, K. (1985): Symptomatic Differences Between the Sexes in Rural Mexico. *Culture, Medicine and Psychiatry* 9(1): 27-59.

GOOD, B., ed. (1987): *Culture Bound Syndromes*, special issue Culture, Medicine and Psychiatry 11(1).

GRIJNS, M. (1987): Tea-Pickers in West Java as Mothers and Workers - Female Work and Women's Jobs. In: LOCHER SCHOLTEN & NIEHOF, pp. 104-120.

HOCH-SMITH, J. & A. SPRING, eds. (1987): *Women in Ritual and Symbolic Roles*. New York: Plenum Press.

HORIKOSHI-ROE, H. (1979): Mental Illness as a Cultural Phenomenon - Public Tolerance and Therapeutic Process Among the Moslem Sundanese in West Java. *Indonesia* 28: 121-138.

KARDAM, N. (1987): Social Theory and Women in Development Policy. *Women and Politics* 7(4): 67-81.

KIMBALL, L.A. & S. CRAIG (1988): Women and Stress in Brunei. In: P. WHELEHAN et al. *Women and Health - Cross-Cultural Perspectives*, pp. 170-183. Massachusetts: Bergin & Garvey.

KLEINMAN, A. (1987): Culture and Clinical Reality - Commentary on Culture-Bound Syndromes and International Disease Classifications. *Culture, Medicine and Psychiatry* 11(1): 49-53.

KLEINMAN, A. (1988): *Rethinking Psychiatry - From Cultural Category to Personal Experience*. New York: The Free Press.

KLEINMAN, A. & B. GOOD (1985): *Culture and Depression - Studies in the Anthropology and Cross-Cultural Psychiatry of Affect and Disorder*. Berkeley: University of California Press.

KRAEPLIN, E. (1974, 1904): Vergleichende Psychiatrie (translated as "Comparative Psychiatry"). In: S.R. HIRSCH & M. SHEPHERD, eds. *Themes and Variations in European Psychiatry*. Bristol: Wright.

KUA, E.H. & A.P. CHYE (1987): *Sanity - Insanity: Myths and Reality of Mental Illness*. Singapore: Times Books International.

KUSUMANTO SETYONEGORO, R. & W.M. ROAN, eds. (1983): *Traditional Healing Practices*. Proceedings, ASEAN Mental Health Teaching Seminar on Traditional Healing. Jakarta, December 1979. Jakarta: Directorate of Mental Health.

LEE, R.L.M. (1981): Structure and Anti-Structure in the Culture-Bound Syndromes - The Malay Case. *Culture, Medicine & Psychiatry* 5(3):233-249.

LEWIS, I. (1971): *Ecstatic Religion*. Middlesex: Penguin Books.

LOCHER SCHOLTEN, E. & A. NIEHOF, eds. (1987): *Indonesian Women in Focus*. Leiden: KITLV.

MARETZKI, T.W. (1981): Culture and Psychopathology in Indonesia. *Transcultural Psychiatric Research Review* 23(4):237-257.

MARETZKI, T.W. (1984): Mental Health Service Development -The Case of Indonesia. In: P.B. PEDERSEN et al, eds. *Mental Health Services - The Cross-Cultural Context*, pp. 221-243. Beverly Hills: Sage.

MARMOT M.G. & S.L. SYME (1976): Acculturation and Coronary Heart Disease in Japanese Americans. *American Journal of Epidemiology* 104: 225-247.

MCDONNELL, K. ed. (1986): *Adverse Effects - Women and the Pharmaceutical Industry.* Penang (Malaysia): International Organization of Consumers Unions.

MITCHELL GUNAWAN, I. (1969): The Socio-Cultural Environment and Mental Disturbance - Three Minangkabau Case Histories. *Indonesia* 7: 123-137.

NAIM, M. (1985): Implications of Merantau for Social Organization in Minangkabau. In: THOMAS & BENDA-BECKMAN, pp. 111-121.

ONG, A. (1988): The Production of Possession - Spirits and The Multinational Corporation in Malaysia. *American Ethnologist* 15(1): 28-43.

PARTRIDGE, W.L. & E.M. Eddy (1987): The Development of Applied Anthropology in America. In: E.M. EDDY & W.L. PARTRIDGE, eds. *Applied Anthropology in America*, pp. 3-59. New York: Columbia University Press.

POSTEL COSTER, E. (1985): *Het omheinde kweekbed - Machtsverhoudingen in de Minangkabause familieroman.* Delft: Eburon.

POSTEL COSTER, E. (1987): The Image of Women in Minangkabau Fiction. In: LOCHER SCHOLTEN & NIEHOF, pp. 225-240.

RACK, P.H. (1985): Review of: Third World Challenge to Psychiatry - Culture Accommodation and Mental Health Care, by H.N. Higginbotham. *Transcultural Psychiatric Research* Review 22(4): 281-284.

RICHTERS, A. (1990a): The Cultural Pathologies of Development: Socio-Cultural Impacts of Development on Mental Health. In: A.A. SALEH & D.F. VAN GIFFEN, eds. *Socio-Cultural Impacts of Development: Some Theoretical Issues,* pp. 76-122. Padang (Indonesia): Andalas University Research Center.

RICHTERS, A. (1990b): Women, Emotions and Disorders in Cross-Cultural Perspective - Between Adjustment and Protest. In: I.M. Foeken, ed. *International Congress on Mental Health Care for Women*, Paperbook nr. III, Between Selfhelp and Professionalism, pp. 37-57. Amsterdam: The Moon.

RICHTERS, A. (1991): *De medisch antropoloog als verteller en vertaler.* Heemstede: Smart.

ROGERS, B. (1981): *The Domestication of Women - Discrimination in Developing Societies.* London: Tavistock.

SALAN, R. & T. Maretzki (1983): Mental Health Services and Traditional Healing in Indonesia - Are the Roles Compatible?. *Culture, Medicine and Psychiatry* 7(4): 377-413.

SANDAY, P.R. (1986): Rape and the Silencing of the Feminine. In: S. TOMASEILLI & R. PORTER, eds. *Rape - An Historical and Social Enquiry*, pp. 84-102. Oxford: Basil Blackwell.

SCHEPER HUGHES, N. & M. LOCK (1986): Speaking Truth to Illness - Metaphors, Reification, and the Pedagogy for Patients. *Medical Anthropology Quarterly* 17(5): 137-140.

SHOWALTER, E. (1987): *The Female Malady - Women, Madness and English Culture, 1830-1980*. London: Virago Press.

SIEGEL, J. (1978): Curing Rites, Dreams, and Domestic Politics in a Sumatran Society. *Glyph* 3: 18-31.

SINNETT, P. & M. WHYTE (1978): Lifestyle, Health and Disease - A Comparison between Papua New Guinea and Australia. *Medical Journal Aust.*, pp. 1-6.

SITOHANG, S. (n.d.): *Child Survival in Indonesia - An Annotated Bibliography.* Jakarta: Atma Jaya Research Centre.

STRATHERN, M. ed. (1987): *Dealing with Inequality - Analysing Gender Relations in Melanesia and Beyond.* Cambridge: Cambridge University Press.

SURYANI, L.K. (1984): Culture and Mental Disorder - The Case of *Bebainan. Culture, Medicine and Psychiatry* 8(1): 95-115.

TANNER, N. & L.L. THOMAS (1985): Rethinking Matriliny - Decision-making and Sex Roles in Minangkabau. In: THOMAS & BENDA-BECKMANN, pp. 45-73.

THOMAS L.L. & F. VON BENDA-BECKMANN, eds. (1985): *Change and Continuity in Minangkabau - Local, Regional, and Historical Perspective on West Sumatra.* Athens, Ohio: Center for International Studies, Ohio University.

ULLRICH, H.E. (1987): A Study of Change and Depression Among Havik Brahmin Women in a South Indian Village. *Culture, Medicine and Psychiatry* 11(3): 261-289.

Anemia, beriberi and rheumatism among the Cabuntogueños of Siargo Island (Philippines)

Norbert Kohnen

Introduction

During nine trips to the Philippines between 1981 and 1998 I conducted field research totalling more than 21 months. Aside from doing research on beliefs and knowledge relating to traditional nedicine I also worked as a physician in the Public Health Centers. I medically examined the inhabitants and treated them in accordance with biomedical and mainstream (scientific) medicine.

History

The governmental Public Health Centers constitute the basis of the Public Health Services of the Philippines. They are found even in the most remote areas today. A big milestone in the country's history of public health was the enactment of Republic Act 1082 (the rural health act). The law envisioned to strengthen the preventive and curative services in the barrios through the establishment of small teams of health workers - and through the creation of so called senior and junior rural health units. Senior rural health units consisted of one municipal health officer as the head of the unit, one public health nurse, one midwife, and one sanitary inspector junior rural health units in contrast consisted of one physician or public health nurse as the head of the unit, and one midwife or sanitary inspector (3 p. 134-135).

In 1953, 81 demonstration units (RHU) were established in selected provinces. Each unit assumed all health activities in the municipality to which they were assigned, demonstrating inegrated health services at the municipal level. To carry out the "basic 7 health services" (maternal and child health, environmental health, communicable disease control, vital statistics, medical care, health education and public health nursing), each unit was provided with a health team. In 1957, 1963 and 1971 some more health programs followed. But apparently successful, the RHU programs were not without problems. Until today quite a number of units are not completely staffed. Specially young physicians left the Philippines to work abroad. So the government send volunteers to the remote areas. But these young physicians don't want to get in personal contact with the indigenous people because of there social status. In most cases I observed the physician did not examiine the patient - unfortunately still a common procedure among physicians and nurses of health centers. They only uncritically accepted the patient's lay-diagnosis and treated him under this diagnosis.

The development of the present system of modern health services in the Philippines was heavily influenced by two health education campaigns. The first was performed by the Americans. In the year the Americans took over the government in the Philippines in 1898, they set up a health committee at the government level. This committee later became an established health institution known as "The Bord of Health" in 1901 - which now is the "Bureau of Health". It not only administered purely medical activities but was also responsible for health education. Campaigns against "ignorance and superstition" were conducted all over the country. Traditional ideas on medicine were to be replaced by scientific knowledge. Attempts were made to enlighten and inform the population at large about the causes of disease and about preventive medicine. School curricula began to include courses on hygiene and on general ways of maintaining and improving health. Trained consultants were sent into the provinces to provide medical education (2 p. 489). Health publications in the form of health bulletins were issued by the Bureau of Health.

One of the results of these medical education campaigns was the adoption of medical terms for certain diseases by the inhabitants. Patients in the rural health center of General Luna (Siargao Island, Surigao del Norte) increasingly claimed to suffer from *anemic* (anemia), *asma* (asthma), *beriberi*, *malarya* (malaria), *nervous* (nervousness), *paralisis* (paralysis), *rabies*, *rheumatism*, *syphilis* and *tibi* (tuberculosis).

105 out of 494 patients (21%) told the Filipino-physician that they suffer from "anemia". An extremely high percentage of about 10% claimed to suffer from "beriberi". While doing so they exactely used these English terms. The staff of the public health station treated them with iron tablets, antihelmetica and vitamins. Because of the extremely high percentage of sufferers from these diseases I started an investigation by intensively questioning the patients.

Beriberi

An example of a literal transcription of one of my interviews shows the problem:

A 54 year old inhabitant of Geneal Luna told me that she was suffering from *beriberi*. The medical examination showed no peripheral neurologic, no cerebral, and no cardiovascular manifestations. Nor could I nor find any other pathological symptoms. The same I did with all the other patients who pretended to suffer from *beriberi*. One in specific I asked:

D (doctor): When in particular do you suffer from beriberi: in the morning, at noon or in the evening?

P (patient): Sometimes in the morning, sometimes at noon and sometimes in the evening.

D: Is there any relation to the meals?

P: No.

D: Do you and your family eat enough in quantity and quality?

P: Yes. - This answer was verified by more questions about the contents of the meals.

D: Is there any relation of your *beriberi* to working? Do you suffer more from *beriberi* before, during or after working?

P: After working.

D: What kind of work do you do and when do the complaints start?

P: Each time after having done the laundry I suffer from "beriberi".

D: In what position are you doing the laundry and how long do you remain in this position.

P: - The patient demonstrated her working position. She explained that she squatted more than 30 minutes without any postural changes in front of a washing bowl.

D: If you get on your feet and walk for a couple of minutes after doing the laundry, do you still suffer from "beriberi"?

P: No.

This example illustrates that the complaints of the patient were not beriberi in the scientific sense but muscular rigidity with stiffness after exertion - or muscle cramps. Without repeating here the clinical signs and symptoms of the true beriberi it is worth mentioning that some of the earliest signs of beriberi are "calf muscle tenderness, difficulty in rising from a squatting position, a quantitative diminution in the vibratory sensation in the toes, and plantar dysestesia." These typical signs are mentioned in the common medical books and surely have been mentioned in the medical education campaigns. The inhabitants probably heard and remembered these concrete signs but did not understand the complexity of the symptomatology of the disease.

Anemia

21% of all patients attending the Rural Health Center on the Island of Siargo claimed to suffer from *anemia*. Only a quarter of them, however, had pale mucous membranes. Intensive questioning of patients revealed that their leading complaints were fainting, tiredness, lack of concentration and sweating. A thorough clinical investigation led to my conclusion that they were sufferers of low blood pressure, i.e. hypotension. This state can lead to the same general symptoms.

The set of symptoms referred to as anemia when attending a physician is locally known as colang dogo, i.e. blood deficiency - a reasonably correct description of the disease. Thus the concrete symptoms were correctly understood - not understood or accepted however was the cause of the disease.

As long as only iron tablets are prescribed (in case of *anemia*) or vitamins (in case of *beri-beri*) only minor negative economic consequences may result. But if physicians or nurses - in order to eradicate intestinal worms as the possible cause of an assumed true anemia - distribute antihelminthic drugs - then negative health consequences can be expected. This is also one possible consequence in case of so-called *rheumatism*.

Rheumatism

The Igorot are an indigenous tribe living in the mountains of the northern part of the island of Luzon. When visiting the health centers they increasingly complain of *rheumatism*. They also look for corresponding medication which they either buy or solicit from the center or the mission. They also do not suffer from rheumatism but from muscle or joint pains due to age-related deteriation and physical excertion. Medication against rheumatism has the disadvantage that it is accompanied by gastrointestinal side-effects such as stomach pains or even stomach ulcers. But gastrointestinal complaints already are highly prevalent in the region even without the ingestion of these drugs. This should alert us to be more careful when prescribing such drugs. Their ingestion in case of self-diagnosed *rheumatism* is not indicated and is deleterious to health.

Traditional knowledge

Additional qualitative and quantitative research about 54 alleged diseases elicited the knowledge people had about the cause and treatment of diseases. It also researched the felt fear, helplessness, pain and threat when faced with a certain disease and ascertained subjective judgements about treatment costs and prognosis (1). The results regarding *beri-beri*, *anemia* and *rheumatism* will be presented below.

Only 54% of the respondents knew that beriberi was due to faulty nutrition. 18% presumed that it was caused by *panohod*, i.e. by cold or cold wind. 24% believed that it derived from general body weakness. The conviction that the disease could be attributed to one's own fault was widely shared. Fear and feeling of helplessness were low, however. Such different attitudes about the cause of the disease show that the information provided by health educators concerning the etiology of beriberi was adopted by only a minority and that indigenous ideas about so-called *beriberi* were blended with scientific knowledge.

Regarding anemia 40% blamed general weakness, 34% mentioned faulty nutrition and 10% believed it to be caused by physical excertion. Among the diseases arising through one's own fault *anemia* ranks first. The fact that feelings of fear and helplessness are extremely low can be attributed to health education. The latter teaches that *anemia* is caused by gastrointestinal worms against which preventive measures and effective medication are available.

In the fishing community of Siargao Island 34% of its inhabitants assume that acute cases of *rheumatism* are caused by physical excertion and 38% believe that chronic cases are caused by *panohod*, i.e. cold winds or common cold. One's own responsibility in bringing about the disease is accepted by many (rank four in a list of 54). Fear and feelings of helplessness figure low.

In sum, all three diseases are attributed to one's own fault and are associated with little fear among the population. These factors are viewed as a consequence of an ingenious health education. On the other hand, the varying ideas about the etiology of the diseases show that indigenous and scientific conceptions have blended.

Results

Well-meant - and doubtlessly necessary - health education campaigns have to be analysed according to the kind of knowledge retained by the population. Only in this way serious damage can be avoided. Experience has taught me that especially the concrete and already well-known symptoms are likely to get linked with new medical disease-labels and then become part of the indigenous language. In other words symptoms are lumped together to a set which has no counterpart in scientific medicine.

The danger of this development does not lie in the labels but in the consequences. The uncritical acceptance of the patient's lay-diagnosis - unfortunately still a common procedure among physicians and nurses of health centers - is responsible for a well-meant but possibly health-damaging therapy. Two types of misunderstandings have to be considered: First the misunderstanding of the layperson who uses a faulty disease label and second the misunderstanding of physician and nurse who uncritically accept the patient's self-diagnosis. Both patient and physician are thus to blame. The unreflected prescription of drugs without diagnostic work-up is irresponsible.

Health education led to the acceptance that personal responsibility plays an important role in many diseases. It also lowered the feelings of anxiety and helplessness towards them. In the domain of etiology, however, it resulted in a blending of indigenous and scientific ideas.

References

1. KOHNEN N. (1986): *Aspekte der traditionellen Medizin in Cabuntog (Siargao Island, Philippinen). Ethnomedizinische Untersuchung zum Krankheitserleben und zur Angst vor Krankheiten in einer philippinischen Gemeinde*. Habilitationsschrift Med. Fak. Univ. Düsseldorf. Düsseldorf 1986.
2. TATE D.J.M. (1979): *The Making of Modern South-East Asia*. Vol.2: Philippinen (p. 421-496). Kuala Lumpur, Oxford, New York, Melbourne (1st edition): Oxford University Press.
3. TIGLAO T. & CRUZ W.L. (1975): *Seven Decades of Public Health in the Philippines (1898-1972)*. Tokyo (1st edition): Seamic.

Midwives in between:
Some thoughts on the training of traditional birth attendants in Samoa, Tonga and Fiji

Christine Loytved

The evaluation of health care strategies always presents a problem for social anthropologists: Hardly anyone dares to advocate traditional cultural concepts of healing when confronted with strong statistical evidence which seems to prove the advantages of "western" medical treatment.

For about twenty years now the World Health Organization (WHO) has been involved in a field that is also subject of social anthropology. While looking for solutions on how to reach "Health for All by the Year 2000", the WHO discovered traditional medicine, concentrating on traditional obstetrics because of its central position in population policy. In keeping with its practical orientation, the WHO developed a training programme for traditional birth attendants (TBA's) based upon its own obstetrical conception. WHO wanted to use the traditional support system but to fill it with "western" obstetrical knowledge and to integrate this construct into public health service in order to reduce financial expenses.

Social anthropology, with its theoretical orientation, has taken a long time to produce any background material, to develop its own ideas about involvement with traditional medicine, or even to discuss the policy of the World Health Organization. Only a few social anthropologists, most of them women, have tried to evaluate this policy (1).

There is very little information about the changes in obstetrics in the South Pacific. Nevertheless, during a research in the South Pacific in 1988, I found enough material on Samoa and Tonga to be able to make some statements about the situation there. Both countries started TBA training programmes quite early their influence spread in the 70s. The results, however, have been different in the two states. The question of whether the changes in obstetrics really do produce better basic health services will be addressed in the following pages, as well as the desirability of introducing a TBA programme in Fiji, where, according to representatives of the Medical Department in Fiji, such a programme is needed.

Traditional childbirth in Samoa, Tonga and Fiji is no longer "traditional" in the full sense of the word. Nevertheless, this term serves well to distinguish it from "modern" or "western" medicine. "Traditional" refers to the kind of obstetrics that was practised from 1900 up until the 1960s outside of the health centers, but which had been influenced by "western" medical concepts. "Traditional birth attendants" seems to be the appropriate term for those who have no western midwife qualifications but who help mothers in "developing countries" during labour. The World Health Organization created this term 15 years ago to define all those persons (lay or traditional specialists) who attend at birth (2). Two aspects of this concept, however, are problematical: 1) The term describes only the work during the period of actual birth and leaves out all of the midwifery tasks performed in the pre and postnatal phases. 2) The term involves some discrimination against the traditional midwives as specialists because it also includes all lay persons who have assisted at birth in any way, as well as separating the traditional midwives from those with full western-style qualifications and should therefore - in my opinion - be abandoned.

Samoa

The Independent State of Western Samoa with its ca. 160,000 inhabitants, consists of the two main islands Savai'i and Upolu and the two small islands Manono and Appolima and has a total land mass of 2842 km^2. Apia on Upolu, with a population of 35,000 inhabitants, is the capital city and the only place with an urban character.

In the literature examined, the practitioners within the field of traditional medicine are not very well distinguished from each other. The practitioners of midwifery are called "taulasea," "fofo," or "fa'atosaga." This divergency in terminology suggests two interpretations: We may not have enough thorough fieldwork data, or that the Samoans may not have a well-defined idea of a midwife-specialist. *Taulasea* is a clearly respectful title for all healers, including midwives. *Fofo* means "massage" and is used for healers specializing in massage for all clients, including pregnant women. The term *fofo* is used - as is *taulasea* - as a term for all healers (3). But when Forsyth (4) asked if the *fofo* also delivers babies, she got this answer from a Samoan woman: "'If she is a *fa'atosaga* otherwise, she only does massage and watches you during your pregnancy. But the baby is always delivered by a *fa'atosaga*.'" The fact that *fa'atosaga* are also *taulasea* show that the specialists treating problems in motherhood are a subgroup of the Samoan traditional healers. We can say that there exist traditional midwives in Samoa called *fa'atosaga* who speak of themselves as midwives and are looked upon as such by their community (5). It has been estimated that 300 persons, mostly women beyond menopause, are involved in traditional obstetrics in Samoa. These healers begin to learn the profession from a relative in early childhood (6). They deliver about half the number of children born in rural areas (7) and are given a chicken or taro, a new shirt or skirt, money and/or fine mats for their services.

Training

In 1968 an early form of the TBA-training programme began when eight young women were trained to be basic health care assistants in a pilot project in Leulumoega district organized by the Samoan government (8). In 1976, 30 women were trained as so called TBA's with support from WHO, UNFPA and Unicef in the demonstration center of Leulumoega (9). In the following two years several four-day training courses were held in the houses of the women's committees or district health centers (10). The TBA-training covered topics such as the reproductive organs, normal delivery, maternal health care, child health and family planning (11). The trainees learned to transfer every pregnant woman under 21 years and over 35 years of age and all "problematical" cases to the hospital (12) the district health nurse was ordered to supervise the work of the "Tba's," who received either no salary or only one *Tala* per month. Each of the 475 participants who passed the final examination got a Unicef-Kit with the basic equipment for a western style delivery (13). The whole programme cost US$ 8,000 - a very low amount for the delivery of health services. But what are the social costs?

Change in the birthing system

Vermeulen, Director General of the Medical Department, stated that only young women without any experience in attending at birth were chosen for the training (14). Only few *fa'atosaga* were actually trained. With some confusion in terms Samoans now distinguish between at least four categories of midwives: Midwives with western school training, *fa'atosaga* with and without TBA training and younger lay women with obstetrical knowledge gained from TBA training programmes. The latter are commonly called "TBA's" by the Samoan public. Only a few of these "artificial TBA's" work as village midwives, because the elder *fa'atosaga* wouldn't allow this competition. Working as a village midwife was not very attractive that's why most of the trainees went to work in a hospital either in Apia or in New Zealand. As there is no statistical evidence for the last statement, we can only assume that the government trained people other than those whom the general WHO policy would have suggested. In this respect the TBA training programmes had no effect on the village level. The *fa'atosaga* kept on working like before. Regarding the number of deliveries, according to official statistics, in 1980 48% of all deliveries were not attended by "trained" health personal (15). Still in 1987 it is said, that more than 50% of the children born in the rural areas are delivered by "TBA's" (16). It seems that the government wanted to distance itself from traditional medicine and to replace it with a western oriented system, but this plan did not lead to success.

The Samoan government has begun to recognize these facts. Since 1987 a new training concept has been developed by representatives of the Samoan Family Welfare Centre. Now the real *fa'atosaga* are invited for one day to stay in the hospital of Apia or in one of the two other main health centers to hear about the importance of registering births and following the main rules of hygiene (17). We can state that there has been a change of policy in Samoa. Up to 1987 the political strategy of the Ministry of Health was to modernize health ideology by dominating traditional values looked upon as folklore or mysticism. Since 1987 we can observe that articulation is aimed at, though the change is to recent as to judge about it's success.

Change in obstetrics can't be discussed without considering the importance of the role women's committees play in the delivery of health services. The *fa'atosaga*, as a member of the committee, can influence the pregnant woman's choice of where to give birth. The Women's Committees provide workspace and accommodation for the district nurse when she comes for antenatal clinic, vaccination or family planning consultation (18). They are a connection between traditional and western health care. Although they receive no official financial help and rely just on fund raising, they are very effective.(19)

If the participants of the meetings now held accept each other as equals there will be a chance for cooperation between the traditional and western system.

The training of *fa'atosaga* appears to be a step in the right direction for the implementation of TBA programmes. However, as is shown in the case of Tonga, this policy can also become problematic.

Tonga

The Kingdom of Tonga, situated next to Samoa and Fiji, consists of more than 170 islands 45 of them are inhabited by approximately 100,000 Tongans. Nuku'alofa, the capital, with about 20,000 inhabitants, is the only urban settlement in the kingdom.

Despite the fact that the different island groups like Ha'apai, Vava'u and the Niuas are spread over 360 000 km^2 of sea, the Tongans can be called a homogeneous ethnic group. Results from one island group can be taken as representative for the situation of Tonga as a whole.

There is only scant information available about the medical system in Tonga and the authors' opinions differ on the question of whether traditional midwives exist or not. Ledyard, an American writer living for over 40 years in Tonga, experienced that every woman in Tonga could function as a midwife. Ikahihifo and Panuve (20) confirmed the existence of traditional midwives, but they were uncertain about calling them specialists as these persons would often practice general medicine too. Bloomfield uses the term "ma'uli" for traditional midwives, as it is also found in the manuals of the Tongan Medical Department (21). These persons, mostly women, call themselves midwives and are regarded as such by their community (22). Therefore we can assume that there is a group of specialists in Tonga whom we can define as traditional midwives. Though many of them are also practicing in other medical branches, they can be called midwives just as we talk of nurses with midwifery qualification as midwives.

The *ma'uli* teach their daughters their skills occasionally a son is trained in obstetrics. The pupils observe their teachers and learn on the job how to prepare the medicines and how to treat the patients. Although healers generally don't accept any salary, they will get presents like kava, tapa, fine mats and food (23). The ma'uli have undergone many years of training in traditional midwifery when they are approached by official TBA-trainers.

Training

In contrast to the Samoan situation, "real" traditional midwives were chosen for the training (24). The main topics of the TBA training programmes in 1966 and 1973 were hygiene, western obstetrical techniques and birth registration (25). Classes dealt with such subjects as diet and behaviour during pregnancy, development of the fetus, anatomy and external palpation (26). The preparation for a western style delivery, bathing of the newborn and bandaging of the new mother's abdomen were demonstrated to the 74 trainees (27). The training in 1973 was especially focused on recognizing high-risk pregnancies, promoting family planning methods and cooperating with other health workers (28). The deliveries made by the trained ma'uli had to be reported to the health centers by the district nurse (29). Delivery in hospital was strongly recommended (30). After having received the Unicef kits for passing the final examination, the only money the trained *ma'uli* can earn from official institutions is the small amount they get from the National Family Planning Association for referring women who agree to use western contraceptive methods (31).

Change in the birthing system

What advantages are there in training the *ma'uli*? Bloomfield (32) suggests that the trained *ma'uli* are highly respected by their clients since they represent an ideal combination of traditional and western obstetrics. But the specially trained *ma'uli* have stopped training their daughters in delivery skills, as they have learned to send most of the women to deliver in the hospital (33) thus, the knowledge about traditional childbirth methods will soon vanish. Instead, the *ma'uli* will keep on working on pre- and postnatal tasks or change to other medical branches. With the training course, they lose their status as independant specialists and work only as supply channels for the district nurses. Most of the pregnant women in Tonga consult the prenatal services in the hospital with mixed feelings. They strongly dislike, for example, lying on the gynaecological chair, possibly even exposed to the eyes of male doctors. But at least one visit to the antenatal clinic seems to be quite useful (34). Therefore many Tongans take advantage of both traditional and western antenatal care.

For the actual birth the situation is different. Many women want to stay at home for delivery and call the *ma'uli* in at the very last minute when hospital transport becomes impossible (35). Both remaining unobserved during labour at home and being frightened at the hospital artificially provoke unnecessary complications for both mother and child.

The situation described above shows the problem in the delivery of health services in childbirth which has been in part evoked by TBA training programmes: The programme, which should have helped to close the gap in basic obstetrical services, has instead created more work for public health workers. Tonga will therefore have more personnel and financial problems.

Fiji

What is the situation like in Fiji? With it's ca. 690,000 inhabitants on about 322 islands, Fiji has a total landmass of 18,376 km^2. Apart from Suva, the capital city with ca. 120,000 inhabitants, there are different towns as Nadi or Lautoka with urban character.

The literature review offers little insight into Fijian midwifery. The main source of information is Waqavonovono's work on traditional medicine and practice in regard to women's ailments (36). As there is no study with participant observation of an actual birth, data are drawn only from government reports and interviews with midwives and their clients.

Official statistics speak of only 3% of all live births delivered by "TBA's" in 1980 (37) with the percentage going up to 12,9% in remote areas (38). Although hospital birth is common in Fiji, pre- and postnatal care is not only a clinical affair. About 1/2 of the Fijian mothers interviewed by Waqavonovono consult both western and traditional midwives in prenatal care (39). Even more use the service of the yalewa vuku (traditional midwife) in postnatal care (40). The mothers deliver in the clinic next to where their own family lives.

Is there any need for TBA training programmes? International organizations like the WHO-Regional Office for the Western Pacific (41) and other recent publications (42) underline the need for programmes which integrate traditional medicine with the official health service. The National Council of Women in Fiji (43) requests the recognition of traditional medical practices and personnel as a health concern issue. Griffen (44) stresses the importance of traditional medical techniques and values. Representatives of the Medical Department favoured the idea of training "TBA's" in rural areas where homebirth still persists. Private or "inofficial" contacts between western trained midwives and their traditional colleagues called "yalewa vuku" in the Fijian tradition and "dai" in the Indian tradition are frequent (45), as Tawake (46) states.

Change in the birthing system

If a training programme with *yalewa vuku* should start, the "conditio sine qua non" would be the interest and willingness of both, midwives and clients to undergo a change. As traditional medical treatment was forbidden by law in Fiji until 1966, traditional healers still feel uneasy when being approached by officials (47). Therefore, in my opinion, a public campaign should be started by the government to reinstate the status of traditional medicine.

For the mothers a change in the obstetrical situation could be helpful. Although it is highly recommended by officials, in my opinion, women no longer want to be forced to give birth in a clinic. Living in a place near hospital for delivery as of the 36th week could be both expensive and tiring. When they move back to their husband in all probability they do not want to experience once more being examined in the lithotomy position by a male doctor in yet another hospital (48). They certainly would like to be in contact with a qualified person in their own home or in a health post nearby who shares their frame of reference. In this way they could be sure that they would be treated in a favourable way during pregnancy and childbirth.

We can further conclude that the *yalewa vuku* are aware of the following dilemma: All their knowledge and advice about pregnancy taboos, massaging and herbal treatments are discouraged by western medical staff, but to stop their medical practice would at the same time mean to negate Fijian tradition and values.

As for the western-trained district nurse-midwives, I would suggest that their interest in traditional medicine is slight, since they only come across the "cases" where local treatment has failed. In addition to this, they surely don't learn traditional obstetrics in their midwifery lessons. As they are used to being regarded as the only "real" midwives they would surely not allow an equal recognition of the *yalewa vuku* as collegues. On the other hand, they would agree to work less while maintaining the same level of authority in the district. The national women's organizations, the village councils, provincial councils and the Medical Department would all surely subscribe to a change in obstetrics even if for totally different reasons, ranging from supporting the self-reliance of women, to expecting financial aid from international organizations.

A change of pattern is required: The superiority of the western medical system, which is still the basis of WHO planning can no longer be accepted. Although it is illusionary to think the theoretical concepts of western and traditional medicine should be combined, cooperation on a practical and equal level could be possible.

These reflections have to be examined through intensive fieldwork investigating traditional as well as western obstetrics in Fiji. This approach should try to avoid neglecting traditional practitioners as in the past in Samoa, when WHO concepts were only used for labeling different health care strategies and/or cutting short traditional treatments without offering substitutes, as in the Tongan example, where following WHO policy still did not lead to the "articulation" of traditional midwives, aspired by WHO health planners.

The field study in Fiji should also evaluate whether the interest of the different institutions involved could be combined or if the present condition doesn't allow for or need any change.

If the reactions are positive, the initiators of the project should avoid determining the contents and form of any exchange of knowledge but should instead only install the framework for a meeting of the representatives from traditional and western medicine on an equal level. Learning from each other's experience could also start in school and during medical apprenticeship.

We as advisors should avoid judging which treatment serves best for which illness. It is better left to the practitioners in the actual case and to appropriate local researchers. Fiji could become an important center of traditional medicine since it is already the home of the University of the South Pacific and the School of Medicine.

Notes

1) Authors, e.g. Jordan (1978), Cosminsky (1978) thoroughly investigate the social costs of TBA training courses.
2) Verderese (1975):p. 7.
3) Kinloch (1985): p. 202; Forsyth (1983): p. 171; Macpherson (1985): p. 9.
4) Forsyth (1983): p.183.
5) The term "fa'atosaga" is also found in the manuals for TBA training programmes of the Ministry of Health in Samoa.
6) As noted by Macpherson (1985: 11), the treatment can involve the following aspects: "(...) massage and manipulation, the manufacture and administration of herbal medicines, the use of various forms of poultice, enema, emetic, inhalation and dressing."
7) Esera (1987): Annual Report, Family Welfare Section. Apia unpublished, p. 2.
8) Samoan Health Department (1968): Annual Report of the Health Department. Apia (unpublished), p. 13.
9) Samoan Health Department (1976): Annual Report of the Health Department. Apia (unpublished), p. 28.

10) Samoan Health Department (1978): Annual Report of the Health Department. Apia (unpublished), p. 53.
11) see (10), p.53.
12) see (10), p.53.
13) World Health Organization (1982): p. 96
14) Kinloch (1985): p. 201.
15) Ministry of Health (1983): Health for all Samoans by the Year 2000. Apia, p. 10.
16) see (7) Esera (1987): p. 2.
17) see (16) p. 2.
18) Gerding (1986): p. 78.
19) Schoeffel (1983): p. 31. She states: "As they (the Women's Committees) receive neither rewards, prestige nor recognition for the many services they provide to the community, there seems a real danger that village women's associations will leave more and more of these services to government to provide. This would cost many millions of dollars and would probably be less effective than the services they replace."
20) Ikahihifo and Panuve (1983): p. 22.
21) Bloomfield (1986): p. 62.
22) see (21) p. 66.
23) see (21) p. 63.
24) Verderese (1973): p. 79.
25) Tongan Ministry of Health (1966): Training of ma'ulis. Nuku'alofa (unpublished). Tongan Ministry of Health 1973: Tentative training programme for ma'ulis. Nuku'alofa (unpublished draft).
26) see (25) Tongan Ministry of Health 1966, p. 4.
27) see (25) Tongan Ministry of Health 1966, p. 5.
28) see (25) Tongan Ministry of Health 1973, p. 1.
29) see (25) Tongan Ministry of Health 1966, p. 5.
30) see (25) Tongan Ministry of Health 1966, p. 6.
31) Bloomfield (1986): p. 77.
32) see (31) p. 89.
33) According to statistics the number of home deliveries dropped from 32% in 1982 to 3% in 1986. Government of Tonga (1982): Report of the Ministry of Health for the year 1982. p. 46. Government of Tonga (1986): Report of the Ministry of Health for the year 1986. p.30.
34) One woman explained to Bloomfield: "'If something happens and you have to go to hospital, when the staff find out that you have not been to the antenatal clinic they would say 'We are not Jesus, this would not happen if you went to the antenatal clinic. If however, a woman did go to the clinic

and the problem was overlooked or not prevented, nothing is said and the staff are more attentive.'" See (1986): p. 90.

35) Bloomfield (1986): p. 90.

36) Waqavonovono (1980).

37) Fijian Ministry of Health (1982): Annual reports for the year 1979 and 1980. Paliamentary Paper 49, Suva, p. 18.

38) Waqavonovono (1980): p. 46.

39) See (38) p. 44.

40) See (38) p. 45.

41) WHO Regional Office for the Western Pacific (1987): Report / Workshop on the role of nursing in PHC, 8.12. - 12.12.1986. Manila, unpublished.

42) See publications as Population, MCH Programmes. In: Health and Development, June 1988.

43) National Council of Women, Fiji (1981): Fiji women's United Nations' mid-decade plan of action 1981-1985. Suva, unpublished, p. 10.

44) Griffen (1983).

45) As I have so far discussed the Polynesian region, I would like to focus - for the purpose of this paper - only on the Fijian traditional midwives yalewa vuku and not on the Indian dai because status, work and world view differ more between Indian and Fijian than between Polynesian and Fijian midwives, as in the past there has been a close contact between the Tongan and Fijian societies and therefore between the two medical systems as well. By the way I would like to stress that given the recent political situation in Fiji, the difficulties of the Indian population should be kept in mind by the investigator.

46) Tawake (1975): p. 35.

47) Waqavonovono (1980): p. 8.

48) See (47) p. 49.

References

BLOOMFIELD S.F. (1986): *"It is Health We want": A conceptional view of traditional health practices in Tonga with special emphasis on maternal child health and family planning.* MA-Thesis in Sociology, University of the South Pacific. Suva (unpublished).

COSMINSKY S. (1978): Childbirth and midwifery on a Guatemalan finca. *Medical Anthropology* 1 (3): 69-104.

FORSYTH C. (1983): *Samoan art of healing: a description and classification of the current practice of the "taulasea" and "fofo".* San Diego.

GERDING H. (1986): *Medizin in Samoa seit Beginn der Kolonialisierung.* Köln.

GRIFFEN V. (1983): *Caring for ourselves. A handbook for Pacific women.* Suva.

IKAHIHIFO T. & M. PANUVE (1983): *Report of a preliminary study of traditional medicine and practices in relation to obstetrical and gynaecological conditions and disorders amongst two communities in Tonga.* Suva: Centre for applied Studies in Development, University of the South Pacific (unpublished).

JORDAN B. (1978): *Birth in four Cultures.* Montreal.

KINLOCH P. (1985): Midwives and Midwifery in Western Samoa. In: PARSONS C. (ed.) *Healing Practices in the South Pacific.* Honolulu.

MACPHERSON C. (1985): Samoan Medicine. In: PARSONS C. (ed.) *Healing Practices in the South Pacific.* Honolulu.

SCHOEFFEL, P. (1983): *Women's associations in the rural economy of the South Pacific: case studies from Western Samoa and the East New Britain Province, Papua New Guinea.* South Pacific Commission Occasional Paper 19, Nouméa.

TAWAKE K. (1975): Role of public health nurse involving women - what to do to make everyone healthy. In: SOUTH PACIFIC COMMISSION (eds.) *Regional Workshop on Future Trends in the Development of Women's Programmes in the South Pacific Region,* Suva 08.19.12.1975. Noumea.

WAQAVONOVONO, M. (1980): *Traditional medicine and practices: An alternative health care system for women.* Suva.

WORLD HEALTH ORGANIZATION (1982): The extention of health service with traditional birth attendants: a decade of progress. *WHO Chronicle* 36 (3).

VERDERESE M. de L. (1975): *The traditional birth attendants in maternal and child health and family planning: a guide to her training and utilization.* Geneva: WHO Offset Publication.

VERDERESE M. de L. (1973): *Report of review and analysis of information and data on traditional birth attendants.* Paper presented on the Consultation on the Role of the Traditional Birth Attendants in Maternal and Child Health and Family Planning. Geneva: 13.20.03.1973 (WHO/HMD/NURS/73.3). Geneva.

The shaman and the doctor - Conflicting systems of interpretation and diagnosis in East Nepal

Martin Gaenszle

Since Nepal opened up its frontier in 1951, a massive flux of aid money has swept the country, of which a good deal was spent on various health programmes. Whereas forty years ago, there were no more than a dozen western-trained doctors, mainly in the capital of Kathmandu, now Nepal has about 450 medical doctors and more than 550 health posts all about the country (1). This is only to indicate what a rapid impact western medicine has had in this specific context: Today, even in the remotest village people have come into contact with the world of allopathic medicine they know of injections and colourful little pills. However, compared to about four hundred to eight hundred thousand traditional healers (2), who still practise their skill and are turned to in crisis, the medical doctor is numerically quite insignificant. Therefore, the question arises: What role does the western approach to illness play for the ordinary villager, and how is it integrated into his worldview?

It is not my intention to answer these general questions in this article. Rather I want to contribute to their clarification by presenting some findings from my own field experience in East Nepal, where I did ethnographic research with onc particular ethnic group, the Rai - or more specifically - the Mewahang Rai. It has been observed by researchers involved in project implementation that generally there are no outright ideological objections against modern medicine (1: 96) and that in many cases both systems - the traditional and the modern - could be successfully combined (2)(3). Viewed "from the outside" such a syncretism may seem promising for a change in basic attitudes. However, as an anthropologist, I am skeptical about a simplistic view of cultural integration, and I think, one should be cautious not to underestimate fundamental differences in the world-views or cultural systems implied. My proposition is that these differences are "cultural" in a totalizing sense: Among the Rai medical knowledge is not just one sub-section of local knowledge, rather it is part of a comprehensive system of ideas and practices that cuts through virtually all spheres of social life.

1. The shaman: interpretation of illness among the Mewahang Rai

The Mewahang Rai of the Arun Valley are one of the various Rai subtribes which all speak more or less distinct languages. They belong - as the Rai in general - to the ancient stratum of Tibeto-Burman populations known as the Kiranti (Nep. *Kirãti*). A main characterictic of Kiranti culture - diverse as it is - is the possession of a rich oral tradition which is generally referred to as "*muddum*". (The pronunciation of this term varies form *mukdum* among the Sunuwar to *mundhum* among the Limbu.) Even though Hindu influence has affected these hill tribes more and more during the last two centuries, the body of myths and ritual texts comprised under the term "*muddum*" has remained relatively untouched. To this day the *muddum* is a major source of the Kiranti's self-perception, it is a distinct heritage which has been handed down by a long line of ancestors since times immemorial. Giving up this tradition would mean to most of them losing their pride and identity (4).

Considering the strong authority of the oral tradition, it is no surprise that the interpretation of illness should be closely linked to it. Most illnesses are attributed to the action of an ancestor deity or an ancestor spirit and in some cases to a living witch or sorcerer. The proper way of dealing with ancestor deities and ancestor spirits is the recitation of *muddum*-texts and the presentation of offerings. To pacify the ancestor deities, the shamanic priest generally goes on a ritual journey to "visit" the deity involved and - after presenting his offerings - enters a kind of dialogue with the deity during which he divines about the condition of the patient. In the case of ancestor spirits, witches and sorcerers, a shamanic medium (Nep. *dhāmi*, *jhãkri*) is required who, with the help of tutelary deities which possess him, can exorcise these evil beings. The duality of ritual specialists is widespread among Kiranti groups (see, e.g., 5), but to simplify the terminology in the context of this article, I will refer to both as shamans. Mythology always forms a meaningful background to these ritual performances as the origins and characteristics of the various harmful beings are recounted in it. What is striking about this view of illness is its being straightforward "interactional". Even when the immediate cause of the illness is seen in some material substance (which usually has to be extracted in the shamanic exorcism), the ultimate source of it is always the malevolent action of another being which has to be dealt with in the proper way.

At this point it has to explained that there is a whole variety of ancestor deities among the Mewahang Rai which are part of classificatory patterns. Some of them are territorial in character, i.e. they are linked to a specific territory which was occupied by a First Settler ancestor. They affect the prosperity and the general well-being of its inhabitants and in some cases also those of neighbouring territories. Another group of the ancestor deities is defined primarily through kinship links: they are associated with specific kinship groups. In general, each ancestor deity is known to be responsible for certain characteristic illnesses. Though the attribution is not always an unambiguous one, it can be said that the classification of illnesses is related to the classification of territorial and kinship groups.

As an illustration, consider the following example. In the village under study, there are three clans which claim descent from the village founder. The senior clan is associated with the cult of *Sarandew* (Nep.), a ritual which requires a symbolic journey to the sky in the vertical line. The illnesses caused by this deity are described as follows: the patient starts to speak like a goat, he tends to become unconscious, stumble on his way, fall down off the trail, inflict burns upon himself etc. These symptoms (which seem to be related to acute shock) are said to appear when the deity is offended, for instance by disregarding certain taboos.

The second of the three clan deities, which is called *Lukwamang* (Mewahang), is conceived of as a snake deity that resides up in the mountains around the border of Nepal and Sikkim where the priest reaches only after a long ritual journey. The illnesses caused by *Lukwamang* are all of an exterior kind: skin infections, especially thoese with pus, itching and swelling. Possibly there is a relationship between *Lukwamang* and the *lu* of Tibetan background (Tib. *klu*, Tamang *lu*) as among the Tamang purulent eruptions of the skin can be caused by the *lu* (6).

The third ancestor or clan deity, *Wayā Nāgi* (Mewahang/Nep.), is also a snake deity. It is a form of the Primeval Snake which initiated the Creation of the living beings in primordial times. The ritual journey in this case follows the course of the river; in fact the priest "travels" inside the river "like a fish". *Wayā Nāgi* is held responsible for pathological symptoms like paralysis, limpness, and also headaches and fevers.

It has to be further explained that these deities not only may affect members of the associated patrilineal clan but also people related to this clan through in-marrying - or out-marrying - women, i.e. through matrifilial links (including patrilineal as well as matrilineal descendants). As all these clans intermarry and the influence of a deity may be effective up to 12 generations, it is easy to see that all ancestor deities are possible candidates for such a causation of illness. It is the task of the shaman to reveal in divination which of the ancestor deities is to be held responsible in a specific case and what ritual action has to follow. Obviously there is considerable scope for interpretation and it depends on the visionary power of the ritual specialist to give a meaningful explanation of the illness. Often also the audience is involved in the process of interpretation and it may take some time until a generally accepted diagnosis is reached (an excellent description of this is given by Sagant (7)).

The threat through maternally related ancestor deities is particularly dangerous in the case of persons whose mothers come from different Rai subtribe than the father. The Mewahang Rai and their neighbours, the Kulunge Rai, for example, both have an important *Nāgi* cult. Both rituals are similar but the snake deities involved are clearly distinguished as each is linked to one subtribe only. So when a Mewahang Rai man marries a Kulunge Rai woman (which is not infrequent) there is considerable ambivalence whether a child resulting from this union will have to pay reverence to the mother's or the father's *Nāgi* - as here only either one *Nāgi* can be regarded as responsible for the child's well-being. It is said that the two *Nāgis* may "fight" for a share of the offerings, the fruit of the harvest which they also control, and the physical result of such a quarrel is illness. For instance, in one case blindness of a young woman was attributed to this kind of ambivalence.

These examples show how illnesses among the Mewahang are often seen to be caused by ancestral forces which are effective through specific kinship links. This gives an idea about the working of this conceptual system: The variety of illnesses is derived from the variety of social relationships. In other words, the diagnostic process by which a certain psycho-physical condition is interpreted, defined and classified draws on the reservoir of classificatory patterns in the social network. As no mechanistic causation is involved here and the multitude of possibilities leaves much ambiguity, the shaman has a wide scope to relate the illnesses to social conditions. Thus, for instance, barrenness of a newly married woman may be related to the negligence of her natal ancestor cults, and the recommended ritual activities not infrequently have a positive effect.

It should be noted that what has been described so far is the ultimate cause of illness but not its immediate cause. The latter is often described in terms of certain "soul" concepts: for instance the "head-soul" is "fallen" instead of standing "high", or it has "escaped" or been "stolen". Therefore, offerings are given to the ancestral beings to "buy back" the "soul". It would lead too far afield to go into these details. Suffice it to say that the condition described as "healthy" is one of "strength" and "power" in the widest sense: it is at the same time political, economical, psychological and physical (see (8) also (9)).

2. The doctor: the role of the health post

With the introduction of various health programmes which brought the establishment of health posts all over the country, the allopathic doctor has appeared on the scene. In many cases, the people accept his treatment, especially in situations of acute problems like those resulting from accidents. No shaman would be sought in the case of an open wound or a broken leg (simple treatment of such cases is common knowledge). In general, the attitude of the people is quite pragmatic and they view both the doctor's as well as the shaman's techniques as useful - both sometimes work, and sometimes don't work. However, a fundamental difference is seen in the methodology and scope of healing as both work on different levels. The shaman's treatment, on the one hand, takes place primarily on a metaphysical plane, and though a physical treatment may also be involved (herbal remedies, magical extractions of substances: Nep. *jhārphuk*), this is encompassed by the conceptual framework of the former. The doctor's treatment, on the other hand, is almost entirely a physical one. Therefore, the latter can be partially integrated into the cultural system of the Rai without too much contradiction. One eats the doctor's pills but still calls the shaman to ensure that the ancestor deity will be pacified.

It becomes clear that the modern medical system is not seen as something entirely unfamiliar which is in competition with the traditional one. Rather, it is given a different status within the traditional system: whereas for the doctor, the modern medical system stands in its own right, being subject only to the laws of natural science, for the Rai it is subordinated to the aetiology of ancestral beings and the concomitant cosmology. If the ancestral forces cannot be controlled, also the medicine cannot work. Thus, the modern medical techniques are often interpreted by the Rai in terms of cultural concepts which give them a different meaning than intended by the doctor who justifies his techniques in terms of the "universal" concepts of science. Sometimes, however, they simply lack a meaning.

These diverging views of modern medical treatment are bound to lead to mutual misconceptions. For example, one doctor told me that people have regarded his diagnostic feeling-the-head of patients with headache and fever as part of the treatment - because it was similar to methods of shamanic treatment. In another case (in an area where attempts were being made to integrate local shamans into the health post) the giving of blood from the finger for blood testing was interpreted as a form of blood sacrifice. In other cases, however, indigenous interpretation fails to detect a meaningful structure. When in the course of a B.C.G. vaccination campaign for children health workers toured the villages they met with widespread resistance: as the injection leads to the development of a little score (and eventually a scar) people could not see any benefit from such a prophylactic treatment. Another problem often complained about by doctors is the lack of cooperation in the long-term treatment of diseases. When medicine should be taken in regular intervals the patient often does so only in the beginning. One reason for this is the common feeling that if the medicine works, it should do so at once. Moreover, as long as there is no indigenous interpretation linked to such continuous treatment, it is meaningless in itself. Especially when the patient is required to finance the long-term treatment himself - as is commonly the case due to the lack of sufficient medicine which the health post can give out for free - he is liable to give up very soon.

On the other side, such misconceptions on behalf of the Rai patients lead to similar misconceptions on behalf of the doctors. These clearly feel superior towards their Rai patients, not only due to their medical knowledge but also due to their role of being part of the national administration. This feeling of superiority is enhanced by the fact that many of the doctors belong to the high-caste Hindus who have superior status within the framework of the Nepalese caste system. In their view the Rai concepts of illness are simply irrational and their culture is often described as "uncivilized" (literally: Nep. *jaṅgali* = 'from the forest'). Contrary to their self-perception, the doctors often face a rather difficult situation in the Rai villages: shortage of food, insufficient housing, lack of authority, not to speak of insufficient staff and medicine.

It is no surprise, then, that despite a partial integration of the two systems, conflicts exist. So what are the conditions under which they appear? As long as the doctor's claim for superiority is ignored and the indigenous system remains intact there is no cause of conflict. But as soon as a situation arises where the authority of the shaman and his interpretative framework is questioned and a clear decision in favour of the doctor's interpretative system is called for, problems are bound to ensue. This usually happens when the health post's treatment requires a more permanent commitment than that of a single or an occasional visit.

As an illustration of the multi-layered difficulties, consider the following example. A young boy around twelve years had fallen seriously ill with what could be diagnosed as tubercular meningitis. Though the boy's condition was getting worse, the parents were reluctant to bring him to the health post which was on the other side of the valley, about 4 hours of walking distance away. Several ritual specialists were called by the parents and there was general agreement on the fact that the boy's "soul" was taken by some other being, though interpretations differed on which being was involved. So, to be on the safe side, various sacrifices to different ancestral deities were offered to "buy back" the "soul". Simultaneously, the father went to the health post to ask the doctor to examine the case. After some time a health worker was sent who looked at the boy and insisted that the boy be brought to the health post - otherwise nothing could be done. An argument ensued between the father and the health worker, who was a young Chetri and had refused to accept food and drink from the Rai host. Though this undermined faith in the capabilities of the health post and the health worker never dared to come back, another health worker could be persuaded to come and give a shot of antibiotics. However, this single treatment was not enough and by this time it was too late anyhow - the boy did not recover.

3. Conclusions: conflicting systems and integration

It seems that the conflict between the indigenous perception of an illness situation and that of the health post arises on at least three different levels.

1. On the **ideological** level there is obviously a sharp contrast of interpretations: whereas for modern medicine curing is a matter of giving the right medical treatment at the right intervals, for the Rai a complex system of ancestor deities and ritual obligations as indicated above is involved. Though the effectiveness of modern medicine is not altogether questioned and its system of treatment may be partially integrated into the traditional view, it is not meaningful in itself. Therefore it has no authority to guide action when traditional habits (such as keeping a patient close to his relatives) have to be given up.

2. This conflict of authority is amplified on the **social** or **interactive** level through the fact that the representative of the health post's approach is often from a different ethnic group, often a high-caste Hindu with different rules for

interaction. Though in principle the Rai have come to accept the purity-based Hindu caste model, today they still feel some bitterness towards high-caste Hindus due to the history of political subjugation and continual encroachment on ancestor land by these "outsiders". Deep inside the common Rai still feels that his ancestral way of life as embodied in the *muddum* is at least on an equal footing with that of the high castes, and after all it's their **own** tradition. For these reasons the boy's father in the example above felt threatened in his cultural identity and rejected the health worker's advice. This only corroborated the latter in his opinion that the Rai are an "uncivilized" people. Here, the importance of faith and authority becomes evident. The value of a medical system is never judged independently of its promulgators: whatever they represent in social interaction, it is crucial for their being trusted and obeyed.

3. Last but not least, the problem is a **practical** one. As usually there are no facilities to accomodate patients at the health post for longer periods. People are unable to stay there unless there are close relatives in the village who can host them. Though some kinship links usually exist between families of such neighbouring villages, one is unwilling or reluctant to be a burden to a more or less distant relative. Also, there is the problem of financing modern medical treatment. As long the medicine is free, patients tend to be more open-minded and keener on experimenting, but if a considerable financal commitment is involved - and this is easily the case in an economy where cash is rare - skepticism prevails.

The importance of each level is variable in different cases of conflict, but generally, it seems, all three are involved. The ideological framework of culture-specific conceptions, however, is always of major significance, if not as a direct cause of conflict at least as an interpretive system for it.

On the other hand, it has become clear that a partial integration of the two systems involved is possible. As soon as the social and practical problems are minimized and a situation of openness and mutual trust exists in which the difference of worldviews is neither emphasized nor ignored but in which common "conceptual schemes" (10) are identified, then a certain degree of harmony can be achieved. Though the ideologies remain fundamentally different there is some scope for "overlapping". This is shown by successful attempts to train shamans in simple medical techniques and use their traditional authority to achieve a better acceptance of the health post's services. By drawing on structural similarities between certain concepts, for instance between "germs" and "spirits", a process of understanding can be initiated. Nevertheless, there is a limit to such translations. Generally, these are only possible as long as the principles of the comprehensive cosmological system remain untouched.

What kind of conclusions can the health planner or any concerned person draw from these observations? Mainly, it should have become evident how important it is to **understand** the indigenous attitudes and concepts and see them as a coherent and complex system of meaning. It will not be of much benefit to overemphasize the contrast of the two systems of interpretation, simply opposing the shaman and the doctor. Nor will it be of much benefit to have a simplistic view of cultural assimilation and integration, thinking that the shaman should easily become a doctor (in the modern sense). Only when the indigenous view is taken seriously and tolerated as something of existential value which cannot be changed just through good advice and services, only when the health worker is prepared to respect his patient's interpretations, will truly "integrated" health schemes with real people's participation be possible.

References

1. JUSTICE J. (1986): *Policies, Plans, & People. Culture and Health Development in Nepal.* Berkeley: University of California Press, pp. 8-9.
2. SHRESTA R.M. & LEDIARD M. (1980): *Faith Healers: A Force for Change.* Kathmandu: Educational Enterprises, pp. 6-7.
3. DHAKAL R., GRAHAM-JONES S. & LOCKETT G. (1986): *Traditional Healers and Primary Health Care in Nepal.* Kathmandu: Save the Children Fund (UK).
4. GAENSZLE M. (1991): *Verwandtschaft und Mythologie bei den Mewahang Rai in Ostnepal.* Stuttgart: Franz Steiner Verlag.
5. FOURNIER A. (1978): The Role of the Priest in Sunuwar Society. In: FISHER J. (ed.) *Himalayan Anthropology - The Indio-Tibetan Interface.* The Hague: Mouton, pp. 167-178.
6. HÖFER A. (1981): *Tamang Ritual Texts I*. Wiesbaden: Franz Steiner Verlag, p. 16.
7. SAGANT Ph. (1987): La cure du chamane et l'interprétation des laïcs. *L'Ethnographie* 83: 100-101, 247-273.
8. SAGANT Ph. (1985): With Head Held High: The House of Ritual and Politics in East Nepal. *Kailash* 12: 3-4.
9. ALLEN N. (1976): Approaches to Illness in the Nepalese Hills. In: LOUDON J.B. (ed.) *Social Anthropology and Medicine.* London, New York, San Francisco: Academic Press, pp. 508-510.
10. POTTER K.H. (1988): Metaphor as Key to Understanding the Thought of Other Speech Communities: In: LARSON G.J. and DEUTSCH E. (eds.) *Interpreting Across Boundaries: New Essays in Comparative Philosophy.* Princeton: Princeton University Press, pp. 21-22.

Ladakh: A pluralistic medical system under acculturation and domination

Alice S. Kuhn

As it is reported from other cultures too, health seeking behaviour of laymen is influenced not only by their individual perception of sickness formed by the culturally determined conception of body and mind, but also by the specific feature of the local health care system. The cultural and emotional aspects of healing with their outstanding significance in the treatment of certain disorders, (for example of so-called "cultural bound syndromes") are not transferable to the biomedical model of allopathy. To provide a population with broad medical help by responding to the cultural and biomedical dimensions of sickness, needs the cooperation between allopathic and traditional healers. The integration of traditional and modern ways of healing, embedded in a general process of acculturation, is attempted in Ladakh/India as it will be shown.

Some facts about the area of research

The ares of research, a part of the Indus valley called "Central Ladakh" (Leh-Block), is situated in the Western Himalayas, a central asiatic alpine region. Its inhabitants are of Tibetan and Indoarian origin and their tongue, belongs to the Sino-tibetan language family. Nowadays, 86% of the population believes in Buddhism, 12% in Islam and 2% are Christians and Hindus (Census 1981, Leh District). Being a kingdom until 1846, Ladakh was conquered by the Maharaja of Jammu & Kashmir. After Indian Independence and the Indo-Pakistan and Indo-Chinese wars in 1947, 1949 and 1962 the international borders were closed and Ladakh became restricted area to foreigners until 1974. Cultural change centering at Leh, started after reforming the traditional law like the prohibition of polyandry by the new state and central government. The establishment of new public administration forms reaching village level and the appointment of non-Ladakhis to highly qualified posts, changed old balances of powers and so became the source of political disturbances till present times. Finally, stationing a primarily non-Ladakhi military force had an ever wider effect on cultural change by developing infrastructure in remote areas. Both military and civil administration became important employers not only for non-Ladakhi immigrants but also for newly recruited Ladakhi soldiers. The majority of the locals however, are still farmers. Thus new (Indian) ideas about lifestyle, modern technology and a lot of unkown consumer goods, were imported. The rise of tourism from 1974 onward led to more foreign infiltration and widening of socio-economical gaps to which Ladakhis reacted repeatedly with open hostility.

The pluralistic structure of the Ladakhian medical system

The Ladakhi "Health Care System" (2) is characterised by medical pluralism and includes the following medical systems:

1. the cosmopolitan medicine (3) (allopathy)
2. the rising popular-culture medicine (4)
3. the folk medicine (4)
4. the traditional Tibetan medicine.

Allopathy was first introduced to Ladakh in 1885 by the Moravian missionaries. 100 years later, it was a manifold system consisting of government and private institutions with qualified and non-qualified medical staff, as well as of institutions of the Indian army and foreign medical organisations. In contrast to the indigenous systems, the cosmopolitan medicine (allopathy) is a "transplanted system" given its peculiar character within the Indian context.

Only 20 years ago the popular-culture medicine arose in Ladakh in the form of persons neither being qualified in cosmopolitan nor in traditional Tibetan medicine such as drugsellers, self appointed "doctors" and also ill-trained Amchi.

The representatives of folk medicine are oracle-healers called Lhamo and Lhapa, which are specialised in curing sickness caused by poison and supernatural powers (demons, witchcraft). Besides that they work as diviners and advisors in common personal matters. Traditional midwives do not exist.

The traditional Tibetan medical system is not uniform. It includes different categories of healers with different degrees of competence, of professionalism and forms of organisation such as: the Amchi (private and government employed), the monks (Lama and Rinpoche) and the astrologers (Tsispa and Onpo). In analogy to them, Islamic healers named Ackon and Shaikh exist as well.

The allopathic medical system

In contrast to British India, allopathy was only recently introduced to Ladakh because of the political circumstances and the exceptional position of the state Jammu & Kaschmir. Arriving in Ladakh, the Moravians were asked to run a small "Western Style Dispensary" after 1885. The first qualified (Moravian) doctor started to work there in 1887. Neither the Maharaja from Jammu &

Kashmir and so indirectly the British, nor the Moravians themselves were primarily interested in providing medical care for the locals. Instead it was of more importance to the government to provide it to the traders travelling from Kahmir to Turkestan and Tibet. For the Moravians, it was a way to propagate their religion. After founding a state dispensary in 1925, the mission hospital became less important and was closed in 1952. In contrast to the mission hospital, the state dispensary had a bad reputation due to illtrained non-Ladakhian medical personnel.

Allopathic medical training at present, is available only outside Ladakh. Being part of the Indian medical system, the governmental health service in Ladakh was structured in the same way but remained under the control of the state Jammu & Kashmir. The influence of the central government is limited to family planning and medical education, as well as to granting working permissions in the medical field.

Until 1985, the administration in Leh-Distrikt was done by Chief Medical Officers. Being of non-Ladakh origin, they were lacking profound knowledge of the specific health problems there, which were and are still different from those in other regions of India (statement of a Ladakhi doctor).

In 1960 only the district hospital, two Ayurvedic and one Unani dispensary existed in Leh-Block. The first Ladakhi doctor trained in allopathy, returned in 1961. In 1970, the number of allopathic institutions had increased: a TB-hospital, two first aid centres and two dispensaries. The Ayurvedic and Unani dispensaries had been changed into allopathic ones, according to Ladakhi informants. Before the opening of the new district hospital in 1980, some allopathic Ladakhi doctors had opened private clinics in Leh-bazar in 1979. A former medical assistant of the Indian army and a medical laboratory technician, followed and offered their services. By 1980 19 medical institutions existed, with 86 employees trained in allopathy run by the government in Leh-Block. Till 1985 the number of medical institutions has increased considerably. The majority of the personnel were still of non-Ladakhian origin and belonged to different areas of Jammu & Kashmir. Villagers reported that till 1980, non-Ladakhi who had been working in most of the peripheral medical institutions, had been absent frequently and unable to speak Ladakhi. This situation has changed because of better means of control and by replacing the personnel with Ladakhis.

Nowadays, in villages with less than 300 inhabitants there are no representatives of allopathy and an Amchi is paid by the governmental health service to provide medical care.

Though medical service in the government institutions is free of charge, only the poorest get it free due to lack of medicine. Wealthy patients are requested to use the private laboratory and to buy the medicine in the bazar. Therefore it is rumoured that the medicine provided in the hospital is of minor quality, an opinion some doctors shared.

In contrast to the 38 villages of the Leh-Block, only in its capital, Leh, private allopathic medical aid is available. The six private clinics are run by an ophthalmologist, a surgeon, a paediatrician, a dentist, a pulmonologist and a specialist for internal medicine. Most of them run their own pharmacy or work together with medicine dealers having bad or no pharmacological education. Only exceptionally poor people get free treatment and medicine in these private clinics. Normally they are sent into the hospital. Most of the doctors running a private clinic are government employees in the district hospital. Home calls are done by most doctors on private basis but only well-off patients can afford it.

The service of the only medical laboratory assistant in the bazar is manifold. Besides his laboratory work,he diagnoses and treates minor diseases and transferes serious cases to the specialists. Poor people have to pay nothing or less money than wealthy patients.

Foreign medical organisations

Since 1979, "Save the Children Fund" (SCF) has been operating in Ladakh in cooperation with the Indian Council for Children Welfare and the Jammu and Kashmir Council for Child Welfare. With the motto "Ladakhi development for Ladakhi", the aim is to give better supply of medical, educational and nutritional help in distant areas. The medical part of the program has included financial support of health workers (mostly Amchi) as well as, training them in allopathic medicine to distinguish serious diseases from other. The health workers have been equipped with certain allopathic medicines, for example antibiotics.

Besides that, SCF has supported the Amchi of Ladakh by founding a library with Tibetan medical texts and by organising Amchi Congresses for further education in Tibetan medicine. Since 1985, SCF has been working together with a "Medical Advisory Board" including staff of the governmental health service als well as Ladakhi doctors, to coordinate the different health strategies.

Besides that, some foreign doctors worked in the small hospital in Choglamsar belonging to the SOS-Children-Village. Due to their different health conceptions and aims, cooperation has not always existed among the foreign doctors and their Ladakhian colleagues. When in 1984 "Medicins sans Frontieres" (MSF) started to operate there, SCF reduced its program for the Tibetan refugees: MSF were running the educational part for Tibetan health workers and SCF was providing the financial means.

The military hospital

After Independence the military hospital in Leh was opened. It provides medical help to soldiers and their families and, in certain cases, to important and well-off Ladakhis as well. The military hospital is said to be well furnished with qualified doctors and good medical equipment.

The popular-culture medicine

Within the past ten years an "underground system of health care" (5) has been developing in Leh-city. This popular-culture medicine is characterised by Ladakhi and non-Ladakhi personnel, neither being qualified in allopathy nor in traditional Tibetan medicine such as drugsellers and self appointed "doctors". More and more shops are found in which anybody can buy allopathic and ayurvedic medicines amongst other things. The customer frequently does not get the prescribed medicine but another one, which differs in substance and dose. Every kind of medicine is available without prescription if asked for. Most of the sellers know about the main indications of the medicine sold, e.g. medicine against coughing, fever and so on. Poor people often are offered single pills for a cheaper price in the market which often belonged to medicine left over from tourists. Here, the sellers mostly do not even know the name and dose of those pills, only that they are against pain, fever etc. They choose them (the pills) according to their colour and shape.

In some cases these medicine sellers give transmuscular injections without caring about sterility. Not only allopathic doctors, but also these merchants, are supervised by agents of different pharmaceutical companies at least twice a year. This increasing engagement of pharmaceutical companies and profit orientation of these healers, is introducing a complete new dimension into the health care system.

Due to the fact that some of the unqualified medicine sellers belong to other regions of Kashmir, their medical concepts are manifold. Characteristic of all of them, is a mixture of different traditional concepts of bodily-functions combined with indigenous and allopathic aetiological concepts of illness (germs, "hot" and "cold" food, harming demons).

The traditional systems of healing

The traditional Tibetan medicine: the Amchi

The main pillar of the traditional systems of healing is the traditional Tibetan medicine (Gso-ba-rig-pa). Its origin is based on different sources (6,7) and it combines elements of Ayurvedic, Chinese and Persian healing traditions, but its characteristic features are those of the northern form of Buddhism. In analogy to the Ayurvedic medicine it can be characterised as a system of the "Great Tradition" of Tibetan culture. As a complex entity the traditional Tibetan medicine includes different categories of healers.

The patient is not seen as a mere case of certain disease but as a sick individuum within his socio-cultural and economical context. The medical training is characterised by a deep student-teacher relationship. Still the basic teachings are the ancient rGuyd bhzi and its explanatory works. The high level standard of Buddhist morality required for the healers, gives them both respect and the possibility to influence their patients on a moral level as well. The training in Ladakh is completed with an examination called tsa Thit, a requirement for being acknowleged as a healer by the villagers. The number of Amchi not having passed the exam is small. Only two out of 56 Amchi living in Leh-Block received a complementary part time education in one of the traditional Tibetan medical centres in India, run by well trained Tibetan Amchi. A traditional medical highschool, as it had existed in Tibet before the Chinese invasion never existed in Ladakh. Before that time some Amchi used to go to Tibet for medical studies. According to the opinion of a leading Ladakhi Amchi, the medical standard of the local Amchis is not very high. From 1985 onwards, it is planned to start a branch of traditional Tibetan medicine in the "School of Buddhist Philosophy" in Choglamsar in response to this problem. Traditionally, healing is performed free of charge. Therefore, all Amchi need the support of their village as well as a second profession to make a living.

According to Ladakhi sources the existence of Amchi in Ladakh dates back to the 11th century. Among 17 Amchi questioned about the duration of their medical family tradition, only one declared himself to be of the 17th Amchi generation which was on record in one of the principal books on Tibetan medicine (rGud bzhi) existing in his library. Most of the other Amchi could remember only three or four generations.

Disregarding the social class every Ladakhi, male and female, can become Amchi. But reality differs: members of the lower classes, such as the blacksmith and musicians (garba, mon and beda) are not accepted, neither by traditional medical teachers nor by patients.

Due to their origin three categories of Amchi exist: Amchi from traditional (gyudpa) families in which the profession is inherited by a son or daughter, Amchi from families without medical tradition getting trained by other Amchi, and buddhist monks who become Amchi during their monastic education. These monks can belong to both family types. Differences in training and later qualifications are due to these facts.

Until the early sixties, Amchi were ignored by the state government and supposed to be quacks. Their integration into the national health system started on the proposal of Dr. Phuntsog, the first Ladakhi being trained in allopathic medicine. Getting a "pocket money" in contrast to the allopathic doctors they had to provide medical aid in villages where allopathic aid was not yet available. In 1985 the Chief Medical Amchi in Leh had to supervise eight Amchi. From 1984 onwards seven other Amchi got supported in a similar way by the British organisation "SCF".

To fight for their interests, all Amchi of Ladakh and Zanskar are organised in the "Amchi-Association", which was founded in 1976 due to the influence of

Bakula Rinpoche, being at that time Member of Parliament in the central government of India. They demanded better financial support by the government of Jammu and Kashmir, pursuit of qualified and further education, research on efficiency of traditional drugs, and better information to Ladakhi people and scientists about the efficiency of Tibetan medicine. Subsequently, in 1979, the central government founded an Amchi research centre in Leh, however under allopathic and ayurvedic guidance. Plans to close this centre and to subsume the traditional Tibetan medicine under the Ayurvedic medicine were fought successfully by the Amchi. Obviously, the majority of the interviewed "Gyudpa-Amchi" showed a tendency towards monopolizing their profession to a limited circle by arguing that "Non-Gyudpa-Amchi", monks-Amchi excluded, are mostly lacking qualified knowledge and understanding of the medical texts as well as of family bound secret teachings.

The main task of an Amchi is described as caring for the general health situation of his village. In reality, the preventic part of the practised Tibetan medicine on village and family level is less than the curative part. The majority of the Amchi practise the psycho-physically oriented field of Tibetan medicine, that means diagnosing and treating diseases with mainly natural causes (food, climate, work). The most important method of diagnosis is the pulse-diagnosis. The main treatment consists of dietary advices, self-made medicaments (herbs, minerals) and moxibustion, to mention only some. Only few Amchi have the ability to practise magico-religious forms of healing or to treat diseases caused by supernatural sources, and few seem to be well trained concerning traditional Tibetan nosology. The knowledge of the majority concerning this branch of medicine, is close to the conceptions of the laity. But they might be good practitioners nevertheless.

The traditional Tibetan medicine: monks and astrologers

In Ladakh magico-religious forms of healing are practised mostly by Buddhist monks (Lama), their abbots (Rinpoche), monks trained in tantrics (Duba) and astrologers (Onpo and Tsispa). Even though their way of practising differs remarkably their source of knowledge is one and the same, namely scriptures of the northern form of Buddhism (Lamaism). Since traditional Tibetan medicine is inseparably interwoven with the teachings of Lamaism, abbots like Rinpoche and well-trained monks always dispose of a certain amount of medical knowledge. Besides the different religious tasks of these healers their fields of activity are to advise, to protect and to remove general damage (notpa, shkyon) and diseases (Doni nat) caused by karma, supernatural powers such as demons and semi-maligne deities. The astrologers, namely the Tsispa, do this by preparing different types of horoscopes, including indications of coming danger or misfortune, designate particular religious practices for protection. To carry out these rituals is the task of an Onpo or a monk. A Tsispa should have profound knowledge of astronomy as well as of astrology. In cases of disease or yearly religious festivals, monks get invited into Buddhist families in order to read special religious texts, for which they get paid. Their qualification varies from ordinary village monks (Chodme), who often can only read the scriptures, to highly trained monks, who are able to perform special rituals. Monks, Onpo and Tsispa generally have in common a distinguished knowledge about demons and deities, their hierarchy, way of harming, kind of caused disease, and way of healing in special. However, the conceptions of some Onpo and monks were nearly identical with those of the laity. The social position of the religious healers is slightly higher than that of the Amchi. In contrast to Amchi or well-trained monks with different degrees, no special qualifications or examinations have to be passed by Tsispa and Onpo.

The profession of a Tsispa and an Onpo is normally transmitted from father to son. In rare cases it is taught by well-trained buddhist monks. Every traditional Onpo-family has knowledge of astrology and secret religious healing traditions (mantra, amulets). Another domain is to diagnose the causes of disease by using different divination books. Mostly the diagnosed disease or harm is due to supernatural powers. Onpo often describe themselves as "lay-monks". Monks having quitted their monasteries and got married are often called Onpo as well. They support their families by doing "Onpo-work". To use "black magic" is forbidden by Buddhist religion. In Ladakh it is said that still two traditional Onpo families have such knowledge and use it.

Superior authority to all of them including Amchi and oracles are Rinpoche of different Buddhist sects (Nyingmapa, Drigungpa, Drukpa). Buddhists and sometimes even Moslems consult them for their advice in delicate personal matters as well as in cases of serious diseases. Besides that, Rinpoche administer ritual purification and blessings, distribute amulets (Shunga) and mantras (sngags). People believe that the Rinpoches power to cure is due to their nature as incarnations and to their excellent monastic education.

The folk medicine

Oracles

The first description about Ladakhi oracles can be found in reports from the Moravian missionaries in the early 19th century: there they are healing disorders of different origin by sucking them out with a pipe. In Ladakh these people are called "luyar" (lus=body; gyar=to lend) because they lend their body to special gods which are acting through them when healing. Not being possessed the "luyar" claim to have no medical knowledge at all. Among the Ladakhis such people are considered to have weak and instable personalities, like "empty rooms".

The vocation of oracles (male: Lhapa; female: Lhamo) can be quite different. Analysing the biographies of seven oracles common to all of them, are indications of difficult personal, intrafamiliar and social situations. In the eyes of the Ladakhis these people suddenly start to behave more and more abnormally, which is mostly interpreted as getting mad or being possessed by witches or demons. In contrast to older oracles it seems that nowadays religious moments in the vocation are becoming much less important. It often takes a long time till new oracles are recognized as such by practising oracles and the Rinpoche. Only thereafter they receive religious teachings from the Rinpoche and a training by a well-known oracle. The duration of the education is determined by the teaching oracle. Before a new oracle is accepted officially by the villagers, she/he has to pass a test to prove to be really possessed by a special god and not pretending to be so.

Lhapa/Lhamo are the most favoured healers among the village people, especially due to the supernatural powers (protecting deities, village gods). The domain of the oracle-healers is multi-various. Due to their abilities to know about past, present and future they give advice for example where to find lost objects, when to start a journey, which kind of rituals are necessary before building a house and so on. Another task is to diagnose diseases and to find out the adequate type of healer. In case of diseases due to poison ("tuk") and harm due to supernatural powers ("notpa") the oracles act as healers by sucking out the poison or by performing magic healing rituals. After being treated without success by an Amchi or a western style doctor, patients often consult the oracles as well. Nevertheless, the oracles are the competent healers to cure animals having eaten needles or other metallic objects.

The healing performances vary from oracle to oracle. They can be performed secretly or with the attendance of other villagers at the patient's, or, as nowadays, at the oracle's house. After getting possessed by one or more deities the performance starts. According to the oracle's teacher the used technique varies: sucking out poison by a pipe, treating by using different kinds of mantra and prayers, divination with the help of barley seeds and so on. Lhapa/Lhamo use their own language which often requires translation and explanation by people familiar with it. In contrast to well educated Amchi the nosological concepts of laity and oracles correspond, especially those regarding "poisoning" and possession due to witchcraft.

Despite the negative aspects of being a "luyar", the oracles are well respected and powerful persons within the village. Due to the deity speaking through them they can recognize witches and point out women giving "poison". They influence the politics in a village and blame people the "luyar" has a quarrel with or doesn't like. Nobody would dare to talk about Lhapa/Lhamo as deceivers, though many are convinced that they are.

Islamic healers: Shaikh and Ackon

In Ladakh Islamic religious teachers are called Ackon and Shaikh. After having studied in Iran/Iraq they sometimes function as religious healers, comparable with the Rinpoche. In the area of research only one Ackon and one Shaikh were famous as healers. Both of them mostly treat diseases due to supernatural powers, such as harm due to spirits and sorcery, with special religious rituals. According to their opinion every kind of supernatural power is one and the same, only names differ due to "Buddhist" or "Islamic" background.

The domination of the cosmopolitan medicine and its influence on the traditional way of healing concerning the indigenious practitioners and patients

As a consequence of the general process of acculturation the health care system of Ladakh was alterated by the progressing domination of the allopathic system. When introducing allopathy to Ladakh no vacuum of health care had existed. The lack of its acceptance until about 1980 was manifold. Allopathy was identified as a representative and product of the government. The new government of Jammu and Kashmir (after Independence) was considered to be successor of the disliked older one. Among traditionally educated people allopathy was labeled as part of a new culture endangering to destroy the indigenous one. Besides that, most allopathic healers had been of non-Ladakhi origin with little understanding of Ladakhi language and culture. Another obstacle was the completely different concept of body, mind, sickness and health among laymen and allopathic trained healers in combination with lack of drugs, corruption, ill trained and rarely present personnel.

The situation started to change when the first Ladakhi doctor trained in allopathy returned and the process of acculturation was not limited to the city-elite any more. The increasing acceptance of allopathy was a result of modern health education in school and army, of the growing number of Ladakhis practising allopathy combined with success in treating infectious diseases and finally of a better communication between patients and Ladakhi doctors. Because the government institutions could not satisfy the rising demand for better medical care, private allopathic practitioners have been establishing themselves successfully from 1980 onwards. Together with drugsellers and semiqualified allopathic practitioners they form a private based system of health care in cooperation with pharmaceutical companies. The commercialization of health is pushed on especially by the representatives of the newly formed popular-culture medicine. They do not hestitate to combine indigenous ways of sickness-perception with pharmaceutical products, to a good deal for their own financial benefit. So a gap between wealthier and poorer patients is resulting.

Until the beginning of the domination of allopathy in the early eighties, the traditional Tibetan medicine had been the main pillar of the Ladakhian health care system. The traditional healers, above all the Amchi, began to react with annoyance to the increasing influence and self-satisfaction of the allopathic representatives. Their reasons were manifold: The depreciation of both their medical knowledge and their methods of treatment as "backward" and "unscientific" by allopathic practitioners, "modern educated" Ladakhis and government employees was considered to harm their function as healers and weakening their social position. Besides that the insufficient education in traditional Tibetan medicine of the majority of the Amchi was criticized. Being aware of this, most Amchi blamed the poor financial support by the state government for it when comparing their situation with those of the allopathically trained doctors. Nearly all Amchi still have to work part-time in different professions to make a living. In their eyes the allopathic practitioners have governmental support in matters of education and jobs as well as a private income. With the introduction of the free governmental health services, most villagers stopped to support their Amchi who traditionally did not charge for diagnosis and treatment but depended upon voluntary support. It is considered to be normal to pay a private allopathic practitioner with money and a village Amchi with "thank you". Only in Leh city the Amchi get paid in money as well. This facts lead to the tendency among young Amchi to migrate from the country to the town. In this way allopathy and traditional Tibetan medicine have come to have a problem in common: the lack of interest of qualified healers to work in rural areas.

Questioned on their evaluation of the efficiency of treatment as well as on their opinion about colleagues of the different healing traditions, the traditional healers nevertheless show a notable tolerance. Allopathy with its new potentialities concerning certain drugs (antibiotics), surgery and obstetrics is regarded as an enrichment for treating especially acute somatical diseases. Psychical and chronical diseases are labeled as the domain of traditional healers, curing not only the symptoms, but the "roots" as well. Astonishingly none of the traditional healers think of allopathy as a superior system of medicine. Amchi and magico-religious healers are of the opinion that the traditional Tibetan medicine is equivalent if not superior to allopathy. The inability to prove this is thought to be due to lack of financial support. Many traditional healers and their patients share the opinion that indigenous Tibetan medicine and drugs are of more benefit for Ladakhis than the foreign allopathy. The majority of the villagers however label none of the existing medical systems as superior. The representatives of allopathy, of Ladakhi and non-Ladakhi origin, however consider the traditional Tibetan medicine to be adjunct and allopathy as the "scientific medicine" to be superior. Magico-religious forms of healing are classified as superstition and as being harmful if patients are prevented from searching for allopathic medical help. Religious healers like monks get rarely criticized because their fields of activity normally does not overlap with those of allopathy.

Inspite of being blamed as deceivers and other severe criticisms, the number of oracle-healers has increased considerably from six in 1950 to 31 in 1985 especially in areas with a fast process of acculturation. This reflects both, a new self-estimation of the oracles with the possibility of a socially accepted treatment of their own combined with gaining influence and increasing income, and on the other hand the increasing uncertainty within the health seeking behaviour of the population. Nowadays the oracle-healer diagnoses and decides whether to see the Amchi or the allopathic doctor. Regarding the change of the health seeking behaviour it is obvious that Amchi and allopathic doctors are both thought to be the competent healers of diseases with natural cause. This assignment stirs up the professional jealousy between Amchi and allopathic doctors.

The dominating structurally superior system of allopathic medicine expresses itself both in the change of behaviour of the patients seeking health, and in the fact that traditional healers are increasingly taking up features of allopathic diagnoses and therapy advice. Integrating the Amchi on the lowest level of the allopathic dominated national health system means a certain control of their resources particularly in asking them to do research about traditional drugs. As long as there is still a shortage of trained allopathic medical personnel in the villages the Amchi will not disappear . Until 1985 it seemed that with the expanding national health service this part of the traditional Tibetan healing system was running the risk of being replaced by the allopathic one. But by 1990 the Amchi-movement has experienced an unexpected considerable revival, resulting in the engagement of some progressive Amchi and favourable allopathic doctors in combination with foreign help organisations.

To observe and analyse the further development of the Ladakhian health care system will be challenging because still little is known about the integrative powers producing its changing shape.

Literature cited

(1) KUHN A.S. (1988): *Heiler und ihre Patienten auf dem Dach der Welt: Ladakh aus ethnomedizinischer Sicht.* Verlag Peter Lang, Frankfurt et al.

(2) KLEINMAN A. (1980): *Patients and Healers in the Context of Culture.* Univ. of California Press, Berkeley.

(3) DUNN F.N. (1976): Traditional Asian Medicine and Cosmopolitan Medicine as Adaptive Systems. In: LESLIE C. (ed.) *Asian Medical Systems.* University of California Press, Berkeley: 133-158.

(4) LESLIE C. (1976): The Ambiguities of Medical Revivalism in Modern India. In: LESLIE C. (ed.) *Asian Medical Systems*. University of California Press, Berkeley: 356-367.

(5) TAYLOR C. (1976): The Place of Indigenous Medical Practitioners in the Modernization of Health Services. In: LESLIE C. (ed.) *Asian Medical Systems*. University of California Press, Berkeley: 285-299.

(6) MEYER F. (1983): *Gso-ba-rig-pa. Le systeme Medical Tibetain.* Centre National de la Recherche Scientifique, Paris.

(7) RECHUNG R. (1976): *Tibetan Medicine.* University of California Press, Berkeley.

Can culture-bound syndromes be regarded as functional syndromes of psychosomatic medicine?

Ludger Albers

When I was doing my work about the South Korean culture-bound syndrome "Naeng" since 1982, I always asked myself what was my position as a western trained medical doctor in the complex relationship between the ill patient with his traditional medical knowledge and behaviour and, on the other hand, modern sciences like anthropology and cosmopolitan medicine.

Only at the preliminary end of my work in 1989 I was able to describe a model which included the scientific backgrounds of the anthropologist and the medical doctor as well as their individual reality in relation to the patient's experience of reality. The most adequate way to get close to the individual reality of a patient, I found, is the psychosomatic approach because it includes organic, psychosocial and environmental aspects of the patient's illness. At the same time it tries always to be aware of the fact that the models created to understand the patient's reality are part of the own scientific background.

Anthropologists who occupy with questions of classification of disease and illness are very often oriented to cosmopolitan medicine because, from their own personal and professional socialization, they have no other criteria for their research and no practical experience with therapy. On the other hand psychosomatic medicine, although it essentially is a cultural science, does not yet have the intercultural perspective of anthropology. So an effective cooperation of anthropology and psychosomatic medicine is urgent.

A basic condition for this cooperation is a strong effort to bring the different individual and scientific realities together in order to create new models for getting closer to the patient's experience of illness. This is an important cultural acitivity which will be of great benefit for every patient.

But there is a big obstacle to reach this aim. Thure von Uexküll wrote in his "theory of medicine" that the construction of reality is - in contrast to animals - a very complex task for every human being because human reality is always ambiguous. One of the strongest factors that determines the construction of cultural programmes of perception and behaviour is the development of phantasy in childhood (von Uexküll/Wesiack 1988a: 271-272). In this sense, von Uexküll describes psychsomatic illnesses as mistakes in constructing individual reality in a certain culture (von Uexküll 1988c: 24).

With the following diagram I would like to present my view of a possible scientific cooperation. It facilitates my task of describing culture-bound syndromes as functional syndromes of psychosomatic classification.

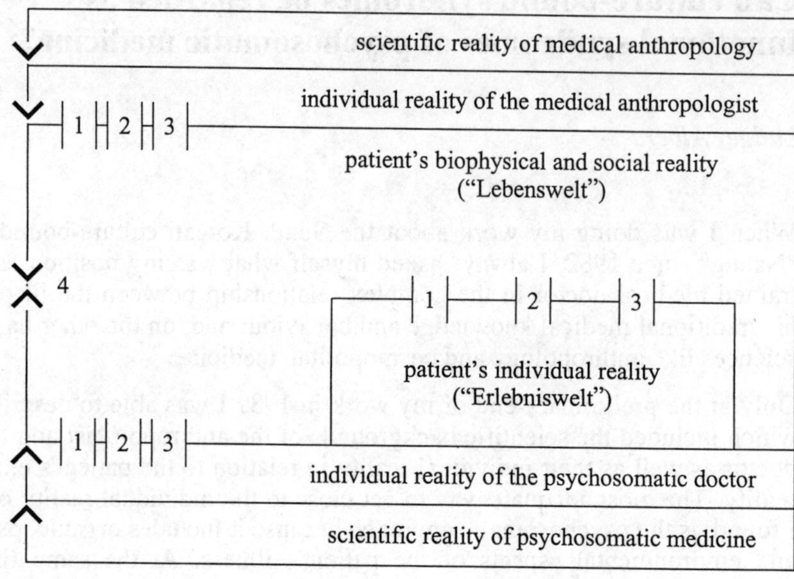

Figure 1: Model of communication between medical anthropology and psychosomatic medicine on the basis of the understanding of scientific, social and individual realities
The exchange of informations (codes) is culture-dependent and takes place in three main ways:

1 = sense organs
2 = language
3 = other ways (feelings, immune reactions, injuries, ...)
4 = place of possible scientific communication between the anthropologist and the psychosomatic doctor

As shown in the diagram, research is always mediated by the individual reality of the researcher who tries to translate the patient's perceptions, thoughts and behaviour into his scientific language by using his personal and professional abilities.

To reach the inner side of the patient's individual reality, the scientist can use his sense organs, his language (or languages) and his feelings. They open him special narrow doors through which he can have a glimpse at the inner world of patients. At the same tine, he can have a look at the biophysical and social conditions that influence the individual reality of a patient from outside. He has to regard that these conditions can have their own development and history.

These facts are important to understand the South Korean lay medical category "Naeng" as a culture-bound syndrome of medical anthropology and, at the same time, as a functional syndrome of psychosomatic medicine. Some of the most important "Naeng"-complaints are: vaginal discharge, back pain, itching of genitals, pain in the lower body, cold hands and feet, headache and so on. It is mostly women who suffer from "Naeng" which means "cold" and gives an important hint to the explanatory models concerning the etiology of this culture-bound states of illness. It is the patient herself who brings the diagnosis of being ill to her physician or to her traditional healer. But modern medicine cannot find organic causes for the patient's complaints and feels helpless, although she does not admit this helplessness (Sich 1979: 87-96).

It was Arthur Rubel who first gave a definition of the folk illness "Susto" as a culture-bound syndrome in hispanic America in 1964. He applied "the prefix "folk" to those illnesses of which orthodox western medicine professes neither understanding nor competence." By his definition, he wanted to describe "a number of seemingly bizarre syndromes which are reported in anthropological, medical, and psychiatric literature from many areas of the world". Rubel stated that physicians, researchers and patients perceived the same conditions from premises about health and illness which were fundamentally divergent. He defined "folk illnesses" as "syndromes from which members of a particular group claim to suffer and for which their culture provides an etiology, diagnosis, preventive measures and regimens of healing." (Rubel 1964: 268)

Cassidy characterizes culture-bound syndromes as follows:

1. It cannot be understood apart from its specific cultural or subcultural context.
2. The etiology summarizes and symbolizes core meanings and behavioural norms of that culture.
3. Diagnosis relies on culture-specific technology as well as ideology.
4. Successful treatment is accomplished only by participants in that culture. (cf. Hahn 1985: 168)

Together with Hahn I would like to support the opinion of conditions highly specific to individuals because I think that culture-bound syndromes nust be understood as parts of lay medicine (popular sector of the medico-cultural system after Kleinman 1980). It is very important to keep in mind that lay medicine usually does not underly any rules of stanardization as they are crucial for modern medicine.

The non-standardized character of lay medical acitvity is the main reason for the "very variety and plasticity of functional symptoms like heart-, stomach-, head-complaints and the vague feeling of being ill without sharp boundaries to conditions like anxiety, restlessness or disgust" (Hoffmann 1987: 182). This is why some anthropologists come to the conclusion that culture-bound syndromes are an artificial product of scientific activity because the syndrome is so much scattered and its parts cannot be brought together to one focussing idea (Greifeld 1985: 273-285).

An important contribution to solve this problem was given by the founder of psychosomatic medicine in Germany, Thure von Uexküll. For him, the often described gap between the state of health and the absence of organic lesions found in the descriptions of culture-bound syndromes was the conclusive hint for the interpretation as functional syndromes which he himself had first described in Germany in 1960 (von Uexküll 1960: 299-340).

A theory of human medicine that understands medicine as a communicative transaction where signs and symbols are exchanged could analyze culture-bound syndromes as efforts of ill people and their social network to give structure to the manifold phenomenons that are relevant for the analysis and treatment of illness in the popular sector of medicine. This theory understands functional syndromes as illnesses which are produced as well by our society as by our medicine as a representative of this society through their special influences on the perception of phenomenons. In this sense, functional syndromes become a "political disease" (von Uexküll 1988b: 8).

I want to give you the example of a man living in an industrialized country and working in an office. Let's assume, in his childhood and later during the period of professional socialization he somehow has learned that he always has to be very accurate to avoid states of anxiety. The fact that this man's behaviour is controlled by this former experience causes a basicly distorted perception which may lead to functional syndromes which are known to be able to imitate all kinds of organic lesions which cannot be verified by the physician with technical methods. It was estimated that about 50 percent of the patients who are treated by a general practitioner suffer from functional syndromes. Everybody is capable of developing functional syndromes in situations of psychosocial stress. In contrast to this, von Uexküll states "that modern biotechnical medicine has become a first-degree risk factor for patients with functional syndromes" because normally the physician ignores the psychosocial background of individual histories (Uexküll 1988b: 3-4). This leads to many technical diagnostic procedures which have certain risks and are very expensive.

But if modern medicine would start to interpret functional (or culture-bound) syndromes "as the consequence and the expression of disharmonies in social interaction" (von Uexküll 1988b: 15) it can take some disharmony from every culture and contribute to the development of a real "cosmopolitan" medicine.

In this sense, I would define culture-bound syndromes as follows:

"Culture-bound syndromes are combinations of physical, psychic, social and other signs (astrological, geophysical, ...)
- which are perceived in a culture specific way by lay people during the experience of illness and
- which are linked to culture specific, but not standardized notions, explanations, feelings, values, expectations, opinions, interpretations and norms
- and this is the reason why only culture specific therapy leads to success." (cf. Albers 1989)

References

GREIFELD Katrin (1985): Susto: Kulturspezifisches Syndrom oder ethnologisches Konstrukt? *Curare* 4: 273-288.

HOFFMANN S.O.; HOCHAPFEL G. (1987): *Einführung in die Neurosenlehre nd Psychosomatische Medizin*. Stuttgart.

HAHN Robert A. (1985): Culture-bound syndromes unbound. *Social Science & Medicine* 21,2: 165-171.

RUBEL Arthur J. (1964): The epidemiology of a folk illness: Susto in Hispanic America. *Ethnology* 3: 268-283.

SICH Dorothea (1979): Naeng. Begegnung mit einer Volkskrankheit in der modernen, frauenärztlichen Sprechstunde in Korea. *Curare* 2: 87-96.

VON UEXKÜLL Thure (1960): Funktionelle Syndrome in psychosomatischer Sicht. *Klinik der Gegenwart* IX/1960, pp. 299-340.

VON UEXKÜLL Thure (1988a): *Patientenkarrieren*. Vortrag im Rahmen einer Sonderveranstaltung der Ärztekammer Hamburg am 19.4.1988.

VON UEXKÜLL Thure (1988b): *Are Functional Syndromes Culture-Bound?* Lecture at the Conference "Anthropologies of Medicine", Hamburg, 5.12.1988.

VON UEXKÜLL Thure; WESIACK Wolfgang (1988): *Theorie der Humanmedizin. Grundlagen ärztlichen Denkens und Handelns*. München.

Medical anthropologists and the study of otherness

Eduard Bonsel

I. Introduction: Don't tell me the truth, so I can believe what I want.

As only one of the innumerable forms of life the biosphere has generated, man lives in a relatively thin atmosphere surrounding a minuscule planet belonging to a inconspicious star which is part of one of the innumerable stellar systems of the universe. Every one of these systems consists of milliards of stars which in seize and temperature are comparable to our sun. In the galaxy of our sun an estimated 40 milliard stars exist, many surrounded by a plethora of planets. The amount of planets of terrestial nature in our galaxy is estimated at more than 600 million. The origin of our galaxy is calculated to be some 4,57 milliard years ago. The life-time of a star as our sun is around 10 milliard years, of which some 5 milliard has passed. The history of man started some 2,5 million years ago when the first hominids started to produce tools. The arrival of homo homo sapiens in the biosphere of our planet was some hundred thousand years ago. That biosphere, as we now understand, is of self-regulative nature, that is to say, it is comparable to a living organism.

As we understand it now, everything anorganic was once organic, and everything organic can be transformed in something anorganic. Animate and inanimate are mutually transformable and unthinkable without each other. Time is the only explanatory category in the biosphere, expressing types of determination often still unknown to us. Understanding what exists, what properties this has, how it behaves, and how it relates to human existence, is a matter of deconstruction. We could call it the archeology of our biosphere.

With this in mind it is easy to accept that it is not given to humans to explain everything there is, was, or will be. The 'thaumazein' (astonishment) of the Greeks and Descartes' doubt ('de omnibus dubitandum est') did not so much reflect man's weakness of character or his lack of knowledge, but the human condition mankind and man is thrown in. Recognizing that we cannot see, define, explain and create everything we want, such limitations do not however, by some natural necessity impoverish the human mind. They enrich it and mark the ongoing evolution of our consciousness as the processing of information in a way totally different from the apperception of unmediated data.

II. No-go areas in western science

Much of the history of western medicine is in fact the history of our ideas about causality. The modern, 'post-Galenic' period started with Galileo Galilei (1564-1642). In his studies in Pisa he met the physiologist and mathematician Gian Alfonzo Borelli (1608-1679), the founding father of the iatro-physical school. Borelli rejected the received views about causality of his time, based on the Ptolemean geocentric view of the world. Views laying at the foundation of medical teaching as it took place at the most important medical faculty of that time in Bologna. When Galilei moved from Pisa to Padua he introduced Borelli's ideas to Santorio Da Capodistria (1561-1636), who refined and corrected this ideas into the iatro-mechanical school. As Padua took Bologna's place as the most important medical centre in Europe, it attracted students from all over Europe, who sooner or later propagated the new paradigm to all corners of the regio. The most famous among them were the Briton W. Harvey, the German F. Hoffman, and the Briton Robert Child, who went from England to the New World and introduced this newthink on the American East Coast.

New in this all was that it slowly replaced traditionally medicine, rooted in botany, by a kind of medicine that followed the new developments in physics. It was through the new ideas about iatro-mechanica that the human body was perceived as a tool, a machine and its workings conceptualized in terms of a mechanism. De Lamettrie's book 'L'Homme machine' (published in 1748 in Leyden, as the author was a student of Boerhaave, one of the leading physicians of that time), had great influence on this development. Notions of plural causality as perceived by the biologist Aristotle and still present in the works of the botanist Linneus (who was a protégée of Boerhaave), slowly disappeared from medical thinking when Newton's (1642-1727) perceptions of event-causality gained general acceptance. Western man entered the period of a rationalistic mechanistic worldview still dominant to date. Causality is perceived as a natural, material necessity, enquiry restricted to 'how, why and what' questions, and explanation a matter of reduction to potential and properties. The 'what for' question, with its intriguing teleological character, essential in Aristotelian biological explanations, disappeared from the agenda or assigned to philosophy and ethics. By eliminating teleology, determination could be reduced to causality of the form: if agens A generates always (the same) effect B, than is A the cause of B, and is consequently prior to B.

Much of the problematic raised here belongs to the debate about positivism and empiricism as part of man's endeavours to find the connections between nature (matter), energy and mind. A tradition in which alchemy, hermetic philosophy, mysticism and the Rosicrucians, Gnosis, Grail, Kabbala, Manicheism, the Templars, Freemasonry, Christian Scientist, Christian Cabala and Theosophy played important roles. In modern jargon one would say it was a search to understand surface appearances in causal relation to the natural structures that generate them and determine their nature and functions. Combined with a theory of production, a structuralist theory of text and a phenomenological sense of knowing, we could call this nowadays 'cultural critic'. Without doubt an enterprise as much persecuted and despised as the alchemists, mystics, etc.

Since the physician William Gilbert published in 1600 his 'De Magnete' about the magnetic properties of the earth as a whole, which book influenced contemporaries like Keppler and Galilei, an empirical, natural science approach to the subject mattter was 'objectively' capable to marginalize and discredit the more speculative, metaphysical approaches. It was in the nineteenth century that this empiricist school finally came home. Men like Ampère, Faraday, Maxwell (who in his electromagnetic theory combined magnetism and electricity) and Hertz, were part of a development that went from 'field theory' to Richard Feinman's quantum-electrodynamic 'unification hypothesis' at the end of the twentieth century.

If such meta(physical?) studies took 'officially' place at all, it was, due to their presumed esoteric character, only in theological faculties. Texts, ideas, notions and concepts expressing the spiritual, once the common issues for debate in, for instance Christianity, became merely subject matter for text analysis. But, this kind of hermeneutics excludes nature, and the 'hard' (positivistic) sciences prefer to side with the devil they know, that is, by using the machine metaphor which guaranteed not only immunity from charges of mysticism, but by perceiving everything spiritual as not 'real', denying that invisable (unreal) powers could influence man.

If we remember that the Enlightenment was a protest movement against speculative metaphysics, we can understand the rationale of this position. This new positivism could certainly be labelled as 'progress' as it defined man (again) as an active, knowing subject, as such liberating him from the passivity of religious bondage. As the early Greeks put politics in the hand of the citizens, the Enlightenment put cognition into their heads. The price of the 'what you see is what you get, and what you get is what you see' epistemology in which that got its form and method, was the reduction of reality to an ensemble of autonomous subjects, which could be known by unmediated (sensory) experience (the epistemic fallacy). It curtailed dynamic relatedness and complex interdependence to linear causality, advocating an amputated type of rationality, unable to grasp all those forces, properties, agencies, processes and determinations beyond direct experience.

This development entailed a profound desinterest in the study about the structural, contingent relations between nature, human body and psyche, culture and society. We know to date from quantum physics that matter, energy, radiation, emanation and causation have more dimensions than being mere equivalents for 'labor', time has more modalities than synchronicity and diachronicity (allochronicity for example), and that in comparison symmetry should be supplemented with eurythmy. We know to date from the study of cognition that reasons are the causes of most of man's behaviour, that his wishes, dreams and intentions about the future determine his actuality (teleology), as his memories or trauma's from the past can do. We know that what is past, or has not yet been are forces man's thoughts and acts are made of and still little serious official study is made about the (iso)morphisms that allow for the processing and interpretation of information within the ecological web man is part of. (1)

It is often said that the failure of the Enlightenment was to put too much weight on rationality as man's only objective epistemological tool to understand and explain complex, multi-form, multi-layered, dynamics of nature and man. Rationality has undoubtedly failed as the perfect instrument for the construction of a civilized world. The sociology of knowledge points out that we have to be careful assessing these opinions. As all knowledge is relative, always a time, place, and concept-bound social construction, we have to acknowledge that for long we were unable to understand the relational nature of rationality properly. But it would be wrong to see the way mechanical causality has influenced our notion of rationality merely as a matter of epistemological inadequacy. The way man was perceived as 'homo rationalis' was as well a matter of ideology, creating a myth to lure him away from feelings and sensuality into a digitalized, moralistic reality. To us, Hegel's view that modern man had set out to free reason from all sensuous concreteness, to enable it to dwell and labour in its own shadowy realm of pure thought and come up with absolute truth, flies in the face of common sense. But this pretense, still rife in certain quarters, has not only alienated western man from his own body, and that of others, it has as well alienated him from other cultures in general.

With a coherent set of cultural, religious and scientific concepts, a semantic and symbolic drug was provided to make man belief that only by suppressing his nature and instincts, he could make reality to its own will. In reality his feelings, wants and desires were of no importance whatsoever for those in power, who had their own agenda about the nature and structure of reality/society. In the field of illness and disease for instance that agenda, by placing culture and society outside brackets, could assign the cause of affliction to the patient himself, calling for self-blame and punishment, and prescribing behavioural change. In case of 'obvious' (sic!) natural causes, fate and misfortune were common in etiology and diagnostics.

To date science and medicine has realized that a purely positivistic approach to questions related to illness and disease, restricting research to physical, biochemical and mechanical causes, is of little or no avail. In particular the old mind-body dualism is replaced by the recognition of the interrelatedness between body, brain and mind.

Nature and man's nature dispose however of many kinds and forms of relationality. Not only more than most languages are able to express with their concepts, symbols, icons, signs, and metonymy. Some even can only be expressed in art, music and dance. Knowledge of other cultures, with other ways and means of expression and information processing make us aware how much man is culturally in bondage. In many non-western cultures simple human acts such as eating or walking for instance have profound symbolic significance. Significance reflecting world views fundamentally different from those constituting western, digitalizing and rationalizing culture. A culture that if push comes to shove still postulates a world subject only to the physical laws of nature. A world in which religion, ethics, feelings and emotions are merely epiphenominal.

It is contingent that only some of the relational equations of our biosphere are within human sensory reach. Much is beyond our sensory, cognitive and scientific potentials. We have no clue whatsoever, whether, and if so, in what way, the 'unknown' influences our bodies and/or minds. This goes as well for many of the relational equations we have (some) 'objective' knowledge of. We know of the existence of magnetic fields, we know that (and sometimes even how) different kind of animals have different ways to use these fields for navigation. Due to the economic and pragmatic nature of evolution, only some of the relational computations that reach our neural system, are transmitted from awareness to our consciousness. Man apparently was equiped by nature with other tools for navigation than using magnetic fields. Our senses can probably detect them, but we can not use them.

We still have little knowledge about the ways our senses filter their input. Just as we know little about the ways and reasons why only some of that input is canalized into what we call knowledge. But we do know why we perceive only a very small amount of that knowledge as 'rational'. Because the sciences have occupied themself (mainly for ideological reasons) much more with who and what man is, than with what and how he feels, western science has developed a very one-sided interest in human cognition. We know for instance very little about the structures that evoke emotions, and even less about the relations between emotions and rationality. That we cannot feel everything we think, nor think everything we feel, has for too long been more a subject for arts, music and literature than for the sciences. Samuel Beckett has pictured this situation unsurpassable:

> Not that Watts felt calm and free and glad, for he did not, and never had done so. But he thought that perhaps he felt calm and free and glad, at least calm and free, or free and glad, or glad and calm, or if not calm and free, or free and glad, or glad and calm, at least calm, or free, or glad, without knowing it. (2)

Only slowly the view gains ground that the realms of the emotive, the sensual and the intuitive should not be seen as mystic, exotic, occult, irrational or feminine, but more as a (normative) challenge to rationality.

If we acknowledge that sensory awareness is the elemental, relational information human consciousness and knowledge is made of, we should admit that there is no (onto)logical, natural necessity to exclude or discriminate emotion and feeling. There may be no proper substitute for rational knowledge, but we certainly can change the scope and nature of it. Just like iatro-mechanics can tell little truth about the workings of the human body, its cognitive counterpart (Humean) positivism, nor (Kantian) rationalism can tell little truth about the products of the human mind. Much knowledge is however not untrue and has to be refuted. It is partly true and has to be revised (constantly). Part of the 'condition humaine' is that we have to live without absolute truths.

We have good reasons to espouse the view that in daily life man produces and applies a mixture of emotive, intuitive, often inexpressible knowledge of all sorts, and objective, rational knowledge. Whether the latter is reflexive and critical depends not only on the cultural and social context it is generated in.

It depends as well on the way and extent we allow emotive and intuitive information to interfere in cognition. Contrary what is generally believed, 'objective' knowledge is less generalizable than what our emotions, feelings and intuitions learn us. The latter seem rather superficial and easy obtainable, but Nietzsche has already pointed out that the superficial often reflects deep-seated human skills and experiences. Man's ratio is juvenile compared to the contextualizing evolutionary experience of his species. A contextualisation our mind is often forced by the presuppositions of culture and the concepts, theories and methods of science, to forgo.

Reshaping views and knowledge of outer and inner worlds is not merely a matter of reworking concepts. It asks for a comprehensive re-fitting of the mind. Questioning the date it obtains, the way they are interpreted, the meaning they get, how they are stored and when they are retrieved. Remaining in one's own culture and scientific paradigms, this is an exercise only few of us, and then only piecemeal can fulfill. It is easier to learn than to unlearn. Confronted with alien cultures, belief systems and scientific paradigms, the task is immense, and usually takes a lifetime. One may wonder whether cultural anthropologists are better equipped for such re-fitting, than others.

The odds are that this is not the case. The old mechanistic and empiricistic views on the metaphysics of nature are still dominant in science in general and in medicine and psychiatry in particular. The social sciences, faced with subject matters combining nature and culture, have until now been little successful in developing a methodological alternative. Cultural anthropology, with its recent focus on text and meaning, still remains in the realms of transcendental idealism, overlooking the epistemic fallacy that reality consists of more than we know and can speak about and the linguistic fallacy that living more than making texts and giving meaning.

III. About medical anthropology

Medical anthropology has put little effort to wrest itself from the methodological traditions of medicine and cultural anthropology. Unable to define properly the nature-culture-nurture character of its subject matter, many of its activities are descriptive, theoretically void or eclectic. Most are mainstream work and sometimes there are good reasons to question the studies. The general character of the work is 'more of the same'.

As the field covers a variety of subject matters, medical anthropology (MA) is a rather vague name for a plethora of activities, theories and methods concerning either the study of the influence of culture on illness, disease, and sickness (MA in medicine) or the study of the influence of culture on the way illness, disease, sickness is conceptualized, diagnosed and treated (MA of medicine). The former could be labelled as discipline-internal, the latter as discipline-external (anthropology of medical knowledge). To some MA is merely descriptive, to others it is a comparative or explanatory discipline. To few it should be mainly a critical-normative study. To some it has a subject matter of its own, to others it is merely an intermediate activity.

Medical anthropology's major activities are in the fields of semantic network studies, explanatory model collection, disease versus illness study, ethnography of clinical events, ethnography of medical institutions, family health study, hidden health care study, impact study, body imagery study, narrative of health and illness study, folk healer study, doctor's versus patient's explanatory model study and collection of oral medical folklore. Those who adhere to what is called the 'political economy of health' approach, focus their attention mainly on the influence of the political culture and economic system on the origins of disease, illness and sickness, and the conceptualization and interpretation of needs. Their critical orientation is the interpretation of origins, meanings and interests.

In all this kind of studies, which often include cross-cultural psychiatry, all kinds of presuppositions of the researchers play an explicit or implicit role. These presupposition are a mixed bag of dominant cultural, social and scientific ideas, and biographic luggage, shaped by education, socialization and experiences of daily life and professional practices. They concern his view about the universe and everything that *is in it*; be it nature, himself, society, culture, or *occurs in it*, be it change, continuity, fate, success, death and too much more to be mentioned here. Acknowledged or not, they determine the way subject matter is choosen and defined, research is done, research findings are interpreted, reported and if possible implemented in policy recommandations. Often quite unintentionally the perception the medical anthropologist has about himself, about the roles he should play in life, and the perception he believes others have of him, colour his research.

The potential to translate presuppositions into dynamic models (metaphors) with the help of language and imagination, allows the anthropologist, like any man, to break free of the constraints of his genes, his history and even his time. He could change his thought models of the past, and enter as yet untrodden fields of research. This freedom is however highly illusionary. Man may be free in his thoughts but most of his actions have to be responses to functional demands prescribed in the cultural, societal and scientific presuppositions of the group he is part of, or (financially) dependent of. If he does not like to be marginalized he has to accept the dominant presuppositions of his society and discipline, as they form the basic ingredients societal consent and prestige is made of.

More than in any other discipline the medical anthropologist is confronted with presuppositions. Propositions which, instead of being valued for their critical and heuristic potential are often transformed and translated into all sorts of prejudices and myths. As the cork on a bottle they then prevent an open and critical exchange with the environment, and consequently hamper the growth of understanding and (self)knowledge. Their main application is then propagandistic, manipulative, exploitative, accusative and oppressive, instead of liberating, enlightening and emancipating.

In the field of health care, disease, illness and sickness, the kind of such myths and prejudices the medical anthropologist encounters, depend on whether responsibility for the affliction is attributed to fate, to the self, to others, or to society. But the cultural and political world views expressed in etiological statements are always in-, or explicitely legitimized by the sciences. Illness then is a multi-purpose metaphor. If, as in the western world is usually the case, the patient is held responsible for his affliction, that metaphor calls for self-critic, self-blame, reproach and punishment, and the therapy for behavioural changes of the patient. If the patient is obviously not responsible for his affliction, he is struck by fate, or bad luck. The machine-metaphor as explanation comes often quite handy in: bad maintenance, inevitable wear and tear, construction failure are all self-evident notions.

If the medical anthropologist follows these phantasmagoric lines of reasoning uncritically, he will reject the use of illness as a metaphor for a harmful culture or society which attacks the individual within its very body. In that case the sick person should be perceived as the exemplary victim, and the researcher should shoulder the task of translating his findings in societal and political concepts and categories. He should be aware that the grammar, concepts and language he is confronted with reflect the dominant presuppositions. Not only do different cultures use different concepts to describe and give meaning to illness, within cultures difference between social classes, and between patients and health care personnel, are normal. Reproach and disdain may confront empathy or care.

In this sense one can perceive cultural, social and scientific presuppositions and the ways they are articulated in structures (society, state, government, politics), institutions (religion, health care), and prescribed behaviour (roles), as iatrogenic. By deconstruction of concepts, explanations, methodologies, anamneses, diagnoses, and therapies, the researcher can lay barren the nature of the presuppositions used. Uncovering ideological bias is however not everybodies cup of tea. Instead of being the spoil-sport in the house, many researchers prefer to paper over social and cultural cracks, defending themselves with the help of cultural pluralism.

Much has of course already been said in the literature about the difficulties one encounters studying alien cultures and people. But much of it restricts itself to abstract philosophical and linguistic problems as they for instance are assembled in the intriguing emic-etic problem. I do not hold that all of that work is a mere swinging of big conceptual punches that don't land. But I do hold that it is often far away from real practical research and too often of little help to construct well-defined research problematic topics. This seems mainly due to lack of multi-, inter-, and meta-disciplinary knowledge and cooperation. As illness or disease is always a conjuncture of causes and forces of different nature, a cooperation of natural and social sciences is an absolute necessity. Most medical anthropological work however is little more than a one-man show.

I will not use more space to flog that old horse but come finally to my main concern. Medical anthropology took wing in response to the bio-, ethno-, and medicocentric presuppositions of tropical medicine and community health-care. And rightly so. Why then one may wonder is so little of that work really mould breaking and thought provoking. Why does it restrict itself so much to the support of introduction and application of western medicine, and why does it contribute so little to the understanding of so many indigenous health care practices?

The answer to me is rather simple: because we do not really want to know and understand what is alien to us. We do not really want to find out whether shamanism has something to do with psychokinesis, whether yoga can be explained with structural morphism, and moxibustion with radionic resonance. We want to refine our knowledge, and spent much energy and money in it. We dream of scientific progress but we are unwilling to go outside the paradigms of our own culture and disciplines. If we are confronted with facts that shake the foundations of western science, we do our best to refute that new knowledge by evaluating it with our old theories or methods.

Received views are constantly protected by our peers, serious articles constantly rejected by anonymous reviewers who belong to the elite of the invisable scientific colleges, concepts are only accepted if they are part of the common jargon of the discipline, research grants only allocated to those who show willing and able to follow the shining path of current research based on current ontology and epistemology. To observe is to see (the gaze), to measure and to weight, reasoning is logic and calculation, concluding should imply predicting, even when we know that everything in nature and in society is contingent, and repetition is not the causal rule but the exception. Much of our learning does not teach understanding.

We in the West have no trouble to acknowledge that the sources of western science are to be found outside the region. But modern science, the best we belief there is, is developed in the western world. It would be hard to admit that some parts of our knowledge is not only very flawed, but very one-sided as well. It would be painful if we had to admit that others probably understand much more about the nature of nature and of man's place in it, than we do. It would be poignant if 'backward' people we have for so long looked down upon, possess more knowledge or better knowledge than we do. It is easier to ridicule and oppose those who try to investigate and prove that.

To understand other cultures and other practices than we in the West are used to, it is necessary to be able to investigate, interpret, criticize and causally explain sameness and otherness at the same time. Necessary but insufficient, as such a person needs as well the intellectual stamina to cope with ridicule and resistance. That task is not light and even hard to describe properly. Western science until now has failed to deal with both, man's inward experiences of the world and his objective scientific descriptions of that world, be it nature or his fellow-man. The study of medical practices as we (still) find them in Asia could help us in that matter. Not just to satisfy our curiosity, or to expose our ignorance, but to finally settle heated debates about the efficacy of so-called 'alternative' medical therapies, over which icy differences have settled. Many of the Witchcraft Ordinance Acts issued by the British in colonial times in Asia and Africa may be revoked there, but such acts still exist in most western countries. That what is exotic is lightly perceived as quackery.

IV. Other cultures, other realities?

As 'culture' is a concept defined in many different ways, the study of culture is still ill-defined. In cultural anthropology we know of more than 150 definitions/descriptions, many of which refer to what is supposed to be good, nice and persuable (civilized), or refer to what is man-made, that is, the totality of products of man's continuous endeavours. The content is either normative, or neutral, while the production of culture is usually explained in a functionalistic way: culture is that what has a function to man and/or society. As culture is used as a model, a system of values, norms, rules and regulations, it is essential for man's feelings of security and stability. Culture as an exclusivistic, normative and paternalistic instrument, is well-suited for identification and expulsion.

Because culture is an all-purpose concept it is open to debate how man should be defined in cross-cultural comparative studies. If we hold that culture determines our rationality and rationality defines our identity, we are, knowing how ethnocentric and scientistic these two concepts usually are defined, reducing man to a machine, some static closed-system (3). Culture's aim, the breeding of cognitive security by rational behaviour may certainly not be denied. But it is the stuff man's cognition is made of that counts. It seems to me, that for the comparative study of culture it is more adequate to hold that every culture is a contingent assembly of tie-symbols, mainly expressing collective, self-made traumas and obsessions (Mayan culture had an obsession for time, others for money), some of these traumas are played out on national level (mainly about war, religion, race), others on personal level (mainly about sex, death, guilt, redemption, power or money).

Such traumas are implicitly presented in presuppositions, of which some make us for instance believe that we are doomed to be the same throughout our lives, while others promise change during our lifetime, in heaven or in some following life. Some see a possibility to change by self-transformation, others only by divine interference. In western idealism man was perceived as perfect by birth but threathened to be perverted during life, in most Eastern philosophies man is not perceived as perfect by birth but able to perfect himself through self-cultivation. As such presuppositions are fundamental to our thoughts and acts, their explanatory value is high.

The same goes for man's ideas about the meaning of life. Contrary to East Asian thought, in the western Judeo-Christian tradition the idea that inner truth is somehow mysteriously connected with some transcendent power, not directly accessible to human beings at large, has long been the truss of much thinking about life and the meaning of life. Secularization has however strongly undermined this presupposition and it is fashionable to date in the West to see life, with its predominantly technological and capitalistic modes of being, merely as 'text' about wars, markets, competition, victory, survival and profit. The dominant emotions expressed in these texts are images about power and money, what they prescribe is treason to reason. It is very problematic for man to survive in that virtual world of illusions and phantasms if he can be certain of himself. By internalizing technology and capitalism with their implicit secrecies, he makes himself immune for criticism, as criticism generates insecurity. As western man is raised, educated and indoctrinated to be an autonomous individual, with solid identity and character, his pride forces him to express his doubts and anxieties (if he has any at all!) only in private. Most of his public discourse, concepts and reports is stripped then from its (inter)subjective nature, reducing spirituality and feelings to functions and processes, unable to reach down to the structural foundations of what it is, how it feels, what it means and what it should mean 'to be human' in the practice of daily life in some culture.

It is doubtful whether in this condition western man is equipped to see, explain, and understand reality and make sensible, documented and argumented judgements about sameness and otherness of cultures, and the way they structure and/or traumatize the lives of those who belong to various cultures. The easy way out is to hold that the world nowadays is a mere 'global village' of jeans, hamburgers, and video-clips. But underneath these signs of progress and modernization at least nine major 'cultures' exist, still dominating the world views and lives of most of its peoples: Judeo-Christian, Islamitic, Japanese, Hinduistic, Confucianistic, Slavonic-Orthodox, Meso-American, Latin-American and African, each of which can be divided in many and different subcultures. Within these (sub)cultures people live often in different time capsules. Some still live in the Stone Age (e.g. on the Andaman and Nicobar isles), some seem on a way back to an intellectual Stone Age, while others are citizens of the post-modern world of productionism and consumerism, or live in a 'time-less' culture of caste and karma.

All have very different presuppositions about the nature of the supranatural, nature, the self, the fellow-man, culture and society, about body, mind, and its various 'beings', and the way man is or should relate himself to that all-embracing context. Presuppositions of which knowledge in the West is often scarce and incomplete. Knowledge according to indigenous scholars too often highly defective and/or deficient. Defective and deficient because the science and language of western culture often has great trouble to understand and/or properly express the presuppositions and concepts of other cultures. Defective and deficient because scholars often projected (unconsciously) their own views into the minds of their 'informants' and then reported this views in 'translation' to their peers.

If most of what we believe to know, to understand and to explain, is merely an ethnocentric product of our culture-bound minds, coloured by the traumas and obsessions of our own cultures, how then do we find out what the difference is that makes the real difference between the ways man perceive their daily realities and behave accordingly. Is there any good reason to believe that the cultural plurality of our world reflects the fact that different, objective realities exist, or is the difference merely a matter of looking different and assessing different what is in essence the same? Does the American saying: 'your home is where your hat hangs' imply that one can change from one way of looking at the world to another, because they are basically the same?

The gap between the kind of statements we would like to make on this subject and the statements actually warranted by empirical evidence is still very wide indeed. Due to the late start of a serious study of cognition and emotion and their interrelatedness, we are only at the beginning of defining what the subject matter of inquiries in this matter would be. Samuel Beckett's observation: 'I only know the city of my childhood, I must have seen others, unbelieving', strongly contradicts anyhow the American saying I just quoted. One wonders whether this difference merely reflects a difference of culture or of something deeper.

V. Different cultures, different men?

From an evolutionary genetic point of view one should hold that as far as our species is concerned there may be 'otherness' but there are no 'others'. There are just different ways of seeing, being, doing, of giving meaning, of 'being', 'being-with' and 'being-for'. According to Parish (4) for the Newars of Nepal, mind, self, and emotion are sacred and moral; the 'inner' world absorbed in a religious ethos. This sacralization of mental life is consistent with the way religious forms - sacred beings and symbols, and a moral order based on a religious worldview - provide the fundamental grounds for the Newar construction of reality.

This sounds familiar to anyone with knowledge about the Judeo-Christian culture. But like I have trouble to understand (= *verstehen*) much or anything at all from western Medieval man or modern Christian creationalists, I have - neither a deist nor an agnosticus, but more of a non-believer - great problems to understand this sacralization as being anything else than a social construction. Belief is of course always something problematic if confronted with description, understanding and explanation. Many even wonder whether belief matches anyhow with understanding in the sense of (rational) explanation. But to me one should separate religious belief from spirituality. The latter is something I have no trouble with.

It is surely interesting to elaborate more in general on this point, but I will restrict myself to the problematic relation between myself as a western researcher and non-western (medical) culture as my subject matter. I am of course conscious about the ethnocentrism and scientism of my western background, its overestimation of rationality and its physical, biological, and psychological reductions of what we do not understand. I have no trouble to show a willing suspension of disbelief, even exhibit (and have) respect for what is told to me about Asian indigenous medical practices. All that may be necessary for my proper understanding, but it is apparently insufficient to change the ways my awarenesses and consciousnesses, and their translations into western ontology and epistemology determine my thoughts and acts. Not that those are always clear to me, but I know often at least what is not clear to me and sometimes even why that is the case.

I became acutely aware of this problem while attending the first World Congress on Oriental Medicine and Yoga (Bangkok 1988). At that general meetings the following indigenous medical practices were presented: Ayurveda -, Siddha-, Unani-, Tibetan-, Holistic-, and Chinese medicine, cold-, herbal-, diet-, ginseng-, hypno-, laser-, magneto- and ultrasonic therapy, acu- and sonopuncture, chiro-practice, homeo-, osteo- and naturopathy, iridology, Kirlian photography, macrobiotics, massage, moxibustion, pulse and tongue diagnosis, and Yoga. In the corridors one could moreover be informed about a plethora of other, less well-known ('alternative'?) therapies and practices. They were applied to medical and mental problems as we know them in the western world and treat them with 'western' medicine, and to problems we do not know, do not acknowledge as being medical or mental problems, or are not certain about.

Although I am no stranger to several of the therapies mentioned, I noticed that my kind of cosmology, beliefs and presuppositions, philosophy of science, theory of knowledge, methodological experience, practical know-how, and concepts, stopped short in really understanding these medical practices.

Diagnosis and therapy were often based on forms of awareness and consciousness very different from my own. Any enquiry I started was fruitless. Any discussion problematic. In most cases I was merely supposed to accept what was told, not to question it. Not that my informants were authoritarian or dogmatic. They just could not understand my questions. As there is often no one-to-one correspondence between symptoms and traditional diagnoses, my informants could tell what they did in their therapies, but could not translate their information into my (western) secular, scientific concepts and ontological modalities. And as so many who practice medical anthropological research abroad, I lacked the knowledge to do this translation (if possible at all!) myself (5).

Contrary to (bio-medical) cosmopolitan (= western) medicine, most of the practices I just mentioned perceive the cause of illness and disease in a combination of pathophysiology and sociopathology. This combination of internalizing and externalizing medical systems indicates that medical practice in Asia is not confined to a well-described social sub-system, but is often an integral part of culture at large. In the western perception it is on the contrary sound medical practice to transfer the patient from the broad realms of bodily sensations and socio-cultural meanings, to the realms of scientific rationality and objective medical knowledge. Disease is then perceived and treated as some abstract entity residing in, but at the same time distinct from the body. Different from Asian indigenous medicine, in most cases no knowledge of the culture and/or the psyche of the patient is required. Even if the affliction is mental, one looks first and foremost in the genes and the brain, instead of using a concept of the patient that ties a bodily, mental and cognitive self to a more comprehensive ecological self, relating nature, culture, society and individual.

Let me use a citation from an article of M.D. Parikh (6) to show how different the western view is from perceptions of the 'self', Asian medical practices reckon with:

> The true nature of each individual is the Spirit or Atman which is the everlasting Reality. When the realisation of one's true nature is veiled by nescience (Atjana) it results in the genesis of individuality called the Soul (Jevaa). This soul takes birth to undergo variety of experiences to remove the nescience and realise its true nature as Spirit (Atman). To realise oneself as the Atman is the true purpose of life. This self-realisation comes about by experiences gained over several lives. To enable the nescient soul (Jevaa) to undergo the requisite experiences in life, it is endowed with two sets of instruments (body and mind) and an agent (ego). It also has a causal body.

I easily confess that at first sight I did not understand that text, and an extensive discursive dialogue with the author could not enlighten me either. On the contrary, things got even worse when it was explained to me that why a particular person was afflicted by a particular disease was a matter of his Prarabdha (fate), that is, not just bad luck, or some decree of God, but the result of his demeritorius deeds in past lives which had not borne fruit at the time of their occurance. So many ontological questions! So many epistemological problems! I know from the history of science that much seemingly incomprehensible ideas turned out to be true. Probably the notion that acts done in former lives can cause disease in the present will one day turn out to be among them. At the moment however I approach, due to the ways I am biologically, culturally, socially and scientifically programmed, this situation under a very different kind of sail. I have great trouble bridging the ontological and epistemological gaps between my reality and the spiritual reality described by Parikh. Like with so many other religious texts to me, it locks up any objective, rational, scientific or explanatory assessment as I know it.

As it is slowly acknowledged in the western world that the exclusion of the spiritual can restrict the nature, scope and depth of diagnoses and consequently the treatment of illness, disease, and sickness, I do not take this lightly. Although the workings of the body are to a large extent independent of the mind, I know that patients always colour their perceptions and feelings, their interpretations and the meaning they give to their disorders and sufferings with spiritual and non-rational notions. That is highly functional, as these interferences of the mind are able to provide hope. But what bothers me is whether this hope is more effective in cultures that take spirituality more serious than the modern western world. Is Asian man different in essence because he can tap forces we in the West do not know of, or have lost entry to?

Hope is of course one of the main cause of the placebo effect as we know it. It is thanks to the cooperation between brain and mind that something utterly immaterial as a belief can have an effect (= cause) on something utterly material as the human body. As hope is one of the essential parts of most religions, it is not surprising that religion and healing are often related, Christianity included. Its basis is the classical notion of 're-creare', create again, make new by coming near (again) to the spiritual, healing source of God.

As an anticipatory, socio-cultural construction hope can however be defined in many ways, spiritual or secular ways, depending on the culture it is generated in. It is obvious that most patients for instance 'hope' to be healed or cured, but what is to be cured or healed, how it will be done, and what meaning it has for the patient, may vary very much. Much hope targets on regaining what was, or having more from what already is, instead of changing that what is. The efficacy of a placebo in the West may be based on the tapping of spiritual powers, but as well on the fact that people are used to live in a world full of technical and natural mysteries they have no knowledge and understanding of. The difference that makes the difference in this matter is whether 'tapping spiritual powers' is not merely a manner of speaking, but refers to a knowledge of reality western man has lost, or even never possessed.

Those who practice medicine, have often to admit that their bio-medical model, with its presuppositions that organic afflictions are universal and its rationalistic and mechanistic views and therapies world-wide applicable, is often at a loss when confronted with exotic, vague, unknown or irrelational symptoms or syndromes. Little we know, and little research has been done to find out whether bio-medicine is really, and in all aspects universal, whether 'other men' need other therapies, or whether indigenous therapies are more efficacious because they relate differently to universal afflictions. Most of the Asian medical systems I mentioned above could be subject to such comparison and much could probably be learned about the natural forces that work on body and mind. Such research is very rare. Not only because the necessary meta-disciplinary knowledge is hardly existing, but I believe as well because it could undermine our western cultural and scientific (presumed) supremacy.

Psychiatry blesses itself that it can label exotic, irrational, strange, incomprehensible symptoms and syndromes as 'culture-bound'. Wind Illness (N. Thailand), Amok (Malaysia, Indonesia), Lateh (Malaysia), Sinking Heart (Punjab), Koro (China), Hwa Byung (Korea), Semen loss (S. Asia), Fox Posession (Japan), Yolmo Sadness (Nepal), Dhat (India), Rampok Macan (Indonesia), Taijin kyofu sho (TKS-phobia of interpersonal relations, Japan) are part of a running debate among psychiatrists whether this kind of possession disorders are real 'disorders' and need treatment, or merely exotic ways of expressing particular cultural feelings or anxieties, and as such below, beyond or above 'real' medical treatment. Culture is then again the 'all-purpose' metaphor that relieves us from honest enquiry and immunizes us for outside critic.

Western psychiatry has two formidable notions to base its diagnosis and therapy upon. For clinical psychiatry that is the 'gene'. If some mental disfunctioning can be ascribed to the genes, society is not to be blamed. For social psychiatry the 'self' is the linchpin for diagnostics and therapy. If something is mentally wrong it is located in the identity. Failures in upbringing, socialization or education, should be corrected by behavioral therapy, resocializing the patient to be better adapted to his environment. Gene and self underline the individualistic perception western culture entertains about man.

Drugs nor behavioural change can really cure bad feelings. And all feelings are the product of man's relatedness. That issue is at the centre of most of the 'culture-bound syndromes' just mentioned. The West has never been very keen to tackle that subject. Contrary to what we are asked to believe, mankind, defined as the totality of man, with its ethical humanistic notion of encompassing social responsibility and solidarity as something to strive for, is in our region a relatively new idea. Comte's 'social engineering', and Marx's idea that mankind can make his own history, were right from the start opposed by so called 'liberal' notions that such 'other-directedness' would give man's autonomy away.

The traditional reflexive 'inner-directedness' of early Christianity slowly gave ground to a Calvinistic 'innerweltliche Askese' which matched well with the capitalist cult of individualism. The only permissable emotional extensions of that 'me-ism' became attitudes like ethnocentrism, nationalism and racism. Man's primordial ontological awareness that his 'being' is always a 'being-with', that all life and living is a matter of ongoing dialectics between subject and object, translated itself into a consciousness and epistemology of insecurity. His world becomes one in which otherness dominates sameness. The result is a militant individualism that undermines the human soul.

Although Asia is not without cultural and social boundaries and cultural and social conflicts, all sorts of traditional totalizing presuppositions still exist. The Japanese 'self' for instance, is commonly perceived as relational, that is, preeminently social, existing in a network of relationships and never autonomously. Relational problems can cause TKS (taijin kyofu sho), a phobia of interpersonal relations. We westerners have trouble perceiving a 'self' structured in such a way that it is vulnerable to TKS. Surely, neither conflict nor collectivity or solidarity are alien to us westerners. But to western psychiatry TKS is something so alien, so exotic, that it can neither properly diagnose nor treat it. If it is mental disorder (at all), it is 'culture-bound' and has to be treated accordingly.

Again we are confronted with the problem whether the ways culture and society canalize man's awareness and consciousness are such that 'other cultures, other men' is merely a matter of mental and cognitive make-up as we know it from the emic-etic debates, or whether there really is a difference that makes a difference, and if so, what this difference is, or could be. Could it be that (some, many??) of the indigenous medical practices I mentioned before, use knowledge and experience about nature and man alien to us because we are more, or in an other way, different from Asians than we want to belief?

In some cases the answer seems simple. Acupuncture is based on a different, less mechanistic, perception of processes within the human body. We can learn this technique, and some even do in a few month. But what about many of the others? Could I learn them and still hold to my western beliefs about nature, man and society? And if I could, would my treatment be efficacious when applied to patients who are products of my culture? I do not know the answers, but I know that Asian healers have no doubt whatsoever to affirm both questions.

There certainly is a practical need for this 'alternative' knowledge. The many failures of western health-care programs, the problems we in the West face when confronted with medical and mental problems of political refugees and asylum seekers and migrants, or with traumatized women who are victims of domestic or organized violence, all show how little we know yet about the religions, belief-systems, philosophies and care-systems of other cultures. How little we know about the ways they influence awarenesses, consciousnesses and identity and how little we understand how these are translated in the feelings, hopes and anxieties, we encounter in illness behavior as we see it in medical and psychiatric practices.

But there also is a theoretical need. It seems to me that by studying Asian medical practices we can improve our knowledge about the ways information is generated, transmitted and processed. Most Asian medicine is after all based on botanical knowledge, and it is, as I wrote at the beginning of this article, that kind of knowledge that because of the development of iatro-mechanics has been pushed aside so much in western medicine. I say 'pushed aside', because if we read Imgard Müller's study of Hildegard von Bingen's treatise about her Cloiser medicine (7), we can see how systematic pharmacognostic knowledge once was. If one compares this book with 'An eight-hundred year old Book of Indian Medicine and Formulas'(8), one is struck by the underlying similarities in the botanic approach.

One should of course not be blind for all the knowledge that remained and the recent interest in plant medicine. But most of this interest is restricted to application. If we see how Resonance therapy, as for instance studied and applied by the Institute for Resonance therapie in Weilerswist (Germany) is perceived by regular science and medicine, we are back to where this article started: iatro-mechanics. Structural isomorphy, the natural path-way for all communication (including transmission of energy), the binding force of all relations, and the intermediary for all processes, is still far beyond the grip of regular science. Knowing the language of nature, knowing the ways it is transmitted, knowing how and when it interferes with the language of man, can shed light on all those mysterious forms of 'contact without contact'. If eyes can express love for one's partner, why could a plant not express its properties the way radionics believes.

Chrono-biology shows the existence of isomorphy between man and his natural environment. The forces of nature are translated into the bio-rythms of the body. Seasonal Affective Disorders (SAD) are a convincing example of their existence. It seems to me that because of the botanical, shamanistic background of most Asian medicine, it has, compared to the mechanical background of western medicine, particularly in that field experience and knowledge to make a difference that really is 'the' difference. Western science has always been obsessed by what 'is', it desects and concentrates more on essence and functions of properties. It is more a science of separate entities than of relations. From a totalistic, ecological point of view, it has to me, still much to learn from other cultures.

VI. Conclusion

If we remember the various activities medical anthropologists are engaged in, as I listed them above, they have a bias toward a cultural mode of thought instead of a medical or biological. And rightly so, as culture can be a forceful explanatory category in the field of disease, health and health-care. But, one may wonder, whether cultural outsiders are able to properly define their research subjects, to understand and to explain their findings, to conceptualize and describe them and to communicate them to their peers back home. One may wonder how for instance we, outsiders, are willing to take distance from the ingrained habits of our minds, from our attitudes, precious products of our awarenesses and consciousnesses. They are good to have, as they warrant a relatively trouble-free reception and processing of the stimuli we receive at home. But are they of any help bridging the immense cultural gaps we (still) are confronted with? What do we do with medical practices based on perceptions of nature, causality, man, mind, identity, views about life, after-life, suffering, fate, duty, guilt and what have you that make real differences between different cultures? Is it possible to find a middle ground between our own attitudinal and cognitive culture-boundness and the necessity to 'go native', that is, to identify ourselves completely with an alien culture? (If that is possible anyhow.) Can we really punch above our weight and free our western consciousness from its mechanistic bondage, to be able to redefine cultural relativity and do away with cultural relativism? Are we able to combine cultural sensitivity and scientific rationality?

As I see it, main-stream medical anthropology is little equipped for such a task. Too often it shuns theoretical reflection in its ardour to prove its applicability, too often it shuns cultural critic out of fear to be marginalized in the own society, too often it shuns out of dilligence for ethnocentrism to criticize the host culture, and too often it neglects the importance of history in its zeal to embrace actualism.

Notes

1. I use ecology in a holistic sense, being the web of relations between nature, between man and nature, between man and his (eventual) supra-natural beings, between man and himself, between man and his fellow-man, his culture and his society.
2. S. Beckett 1963: Watt. John Calden, London, p. 133.
3. We know of at least seven different identity theories:
   - empiricistic bundel theory (Quinton)
   - metaphysical ego theory (Chisholm)
   - body theory (B. Williams)
   - brain theory (J.L. Mackie)
   - subjectivity theory (T. Nagel)
   - persons theory (P.F. Strawson)
   - theory of man (L. Wittgenstein).
4. S.M. Parish 1991: The Sacred Mind: Newar Cultural Representations of Mental Life and the Production of Moral Consciousness. In: Ethos 19/3, p. 313.

5. Scholars like Paul Unschuld (Germany), Francis Zimmerman (France) and Jan Meulenbelt (The Netherlands) come to mind here. They combine knowledge of the 'hard sciences' with cultural and linguistic knowledge of (parts of) Asia.
6. M.D. Parikh 1988: Composition of Human Being: A Holistic Concept. In: The J. of Res. & Ed. in Indian Medicine, Vol. VII(1), p. 67.
7. I. Müller 1993: Die pflanzlichen Heilmittel bei Hildegard von Bingen: Heilwissen aus der Klostermedizin, Herder Verlag.
8. Translated from the original very old Hindi into Gujarati character and thence into English by Elizabeth Sharpe 1937, London, Luzac & Co.

Background literature

Books

CHENNAKESAVAN S. (1960): *Concepts of Mind in Indian Philosophy*. Motilal Banarsidass: Delhi.

DANIEL J.MC. (1989): *The Madness of Saints: Ecstatic Religion in Bengal*. University of Chicago Press: Chicago/London.

DASGUPTA S. (1987): *Natural Science of the Ancient Hindus*. Motilal Banarsidass: Delhi.

GEERTZ C. (1973): *The Interpretation of Cultures*. Basic Books: New York.

HIRIYANNA M. (1973): *Outlines of Indian Philosophy*. Allen & Unwin: London 1932.

HOFFMAN F.J. (1987): *Rationality and Mind in Early Buddhism*. Motilal Banarsidass: Delhi.

LARSON G.J. & E. DEUTSCH, eds. (1989): *Interpreting across Boundaries: New Essays in Comparative Philosophy*. Princeton University Press: Princeton 1988, reprint Motilal Banarsidass: Delhi.

MARSELLA A.J., G. DEVOS & F.L.K. HU (1985): *Culture and Self: Asian and Western Perspectives*. Tavistock: New York/London.

SCHARFSTEIN B.-A., ed. (1978): *Philosophy East - Philosophy West: A Critical Comparison of Indian, Chinese, Islamic and European Philosophy*. Blackwell: Oxford.

SEAL B. (1985): *The Positive Sciences of the Ancient Hindus*. Motilal Banarsidass: Delhi.

SMART N. (1964): *Doctrine and Argument in Indian Philosophy*. Allen: London.

THAKKUR C.G. (1981): *Ayurveda: The Indian Art & Science of Medicine*. ASI Publishers: New York.

Articles about culture-bound syndromes

CARR J.E. (1978): Ethno-Behaviorism and the Culture-bound Syndromes: The Case of Amok. *Culture, Medicine & Psychiatry* 2(3): 269-294.

DESJARLAIS R.R. (1991): Poetic Transformation of Yolmo 'Sadness'. *Culture, Medicine & Psychiatry* 15(4): 387-421

DEWARAJA R. & Y. SASAKI (1991): Semenloss Syndrome: A Comparison between Sri Lanka and Japan. *American Journal of Psychotherapy* 45: 14-20.

EDWARD J.W. (1983): Semen Anxiety in South Asian Cultures: Cultural and Transcultural Significance. *Medical Anthropology* 7(3): 51-68.

EGUCHI S. (1991): Between Folk Concepts of Illness and Psychiatric Diagnosis: Kitsune-Tsuki (Fox Possession) in a Mountain Village of Western Japan. *Culture, Medicine & Psychiatry* 15(4): 421-453.

KRAUSE Inga-Britt (1989): Sinking Heart: A Punjabi Communication Distress. *Social Science & Medicine* 29(4): 563-577.

LIN K.M. (1983): Hwa-Byung: A Korean Culture-Bound Syndrome?. *American Journal of Psychiatry* 240: 105-107.

MUECKE Majorie A. (1979): An explication of 'Wind Illness' in Northern Thailand. *Culture, Medicine & Psychiatry* 3(3): 267-301.

PRINCE R.H. (1989): A Review of three Papers on Culture-bound Syndromes in South East Asia. *Transcultural Psychiatric Research Review* 26(2): 137-148.

SINGH G. (1985): Dhat Syndrome Revisited. *Indian Journal of Psychiatry* 27: 119-122.

TSENG W-S. et al. (1988): A Socio-cultural and Clinical Study of Koro (Genital Retraction Panic Disorder) Epidemic in Guangdong, China. *Transcultural Psychiatric Research Review* 25(1): 74-78.

WESSING R. (1992): A Tiger in the Heart: The Javanese 'Rampok Macan'. *Bijdrage Taal, Land en Volkenkunde* 148(2): 287-309.

Index

Beiträge zur Südasienforschung

Stuttgart: Steiner

ISSN 0170-3137

Abbreviation: BSAF

127 Reduplizierte Verbstämme im Tamil / von *Thomas Malten*. – 1989. IX, 283 S. ISBN 3-515-05378-6

128 Islamisierung in Pakistan, 1977 - 1984 : Untersuchungen zu autochthonen Strukturen / von *S. Jamal Malik*. – 1989. XVII, 475 S. ISBN 3-515-05389-1

129 Banks, gods and government : institutional and informal credit structure in a remote and tribal Indian district (Kinnaur, Himachal Pradesh) ; 1960 - 1985 / by *Jogishwar Singh*. – 1989. XXXVIII, 410 p. ISBN 3-515-05396-4

130 Galle : geomedizinische Analyse einer Küstenstadt auf Sri Lanka (Ceylon) / von *Hella Wellmer*. – 1989. XXXIV, 557 S. ISBN 3-515-05444-8

131 Die Geschichte der United National Party in Sri Lanka / von *Thomas Prinz*. – 1989. XXVII, 274 S. ISBN 3-515-05567-3

132 Bhakti und Bhakta : religionsgeschichtliche Untersuchungen zum Heilsbegriff und zur religiösen Umwelt des Śrī Sant Ekanāth / von *Hugh van Skyhawk*. – 1990. XVI, 382 S. ISBN 3-515-05618-1

133 Zielgruppenorientierte Ernährungspolitik für Entwicklungsländer : empirische Sektoranalyse auf der Basis ökonometrischer Nachfrage- und Angebotssysteme am Beispiel Indonesiens / von *Serge-Arno Klümper*. – 1990. XVI, 580 S. ISBN 3-515-05620-3

134 Die frühere Sozialordnung Moolkhos und Turkhos (Chitral) / von *Peter Eggert*. – 1990. VII, 271 S. ISBN 3-515-05735-8

135 *Erste Heidelberger Südasiengespräche* / hrsg. von Dietmar Rothermund. – 1990. IX, 125 S. ISBN 3-515-05804-4

136 Verwandtschaft und Mythologie bei den Mewahang Rai in Ostnepal : eine ethnographische Studie zum Problem der 'ethnischen Identität' / von *Martin Gaenszle*. – 1991. XV, 409 S. ISBN 3-515-05861-3

137 *Political transition in South Asia* : regional cooperation, ethnic conflict, political participation. / ed. by Dagmar Bernstorff ; Dieter Braun. – 1991. XVI, 168 p. ISBN 3-515-05886-9

138 *Dādū* : Lieder / übersetzt von Monika Thiel-Horstmann. – 1991. XIII, 388 S. ISBN 3-515-05421-9

139 Das Hindukush-Haus : zum symbolischen Prinzip der Sonderstellung von Raummitte und Raumhintergrund / von *Dieter Walter Illi*. – 1991. 299 S., 48 Taf., Kt. ISBN 3-515-05932-6

140 *Südasienanthologie* : 44 Übersetzungen aus südasiatischen Literaturen / hrsg. von Günther D. Sontheimer in Zusammenarbeit mit Helma Werny. – 1993. XIV, 306 S., Kt. ISBN 3-515-06025-1

141 *Emporia, commodities and entrepreneurs in Asian maritime trade*, c. 1400 - 1750 / ed. by Roderich Ptak and Dietmar Rothermund. – 1991. XI, 509 p. ISBN 3-515-05962-8

142 Materials for an edition and study of the Piṇḍa- and Oha-Nijjuttis of the Śvetāmbara Jain tradition / *Willem B. Bollée*.
(1. Pāda indices.) – 1991. XV, 160 p. ISBN 3-515-05794-3

143 Veda-Lakṣaṇa. Vedic ancillary literature : a descriptive bibliography / compiled by *K. Parameswara Aithal.* – 1991. II, 725 p. ISBN 3-515-05795-1

144 Die Sprachenpolitik der Muslim-League-Regierung und die Entstehung der Bengali-Sprachbewegung in Ostbengalen, 1947 - 1956 / von *Satya N. Bhowmik.* – 1993. XII, 408 S. ISBN 3-515-06383-8

145 *Islam and Indian regions* / ed. by Anna Libera Dallapiccola and Stephanie Zingel-Avé Lallemant. – 1992. ISBN 3-515-06272-6
Vol.1. Texts. – XI, 553 p.
Vol.2. Index, bibliography, illustrations. – VI, 118 p., plates.

146 Nuwara Eliya : 'Hill station' und zentraler Ort im Hochland der Insel Ceylon (Sri Lanka) / von *Monika Bührlein.* – 1991. XXXII, 476 S., 44 Taf. ISBN 3-515-06035-9

147 A word index of old Tamil caṅkam literature / by *Thomas Lehmann* and *Thomas Malten.* – 1992. X, 425 p. ISBN 3-515-05814-1

148 Britische Herrschaft auf indischem Boden : landwirtschaftliche Transformation und ökologische Destruktion des 'Central Doab' ; 1801 - 1854 / von *Michael Mann.* – 1992. IX, 240 S. ISBN 3-515-06125-8

149 *Nationalstaat und Sprachkonflikte in Süd- und Südostasien* / hrsg. von Dagmar Hellmann-Rajanayagam und Dietmar Rothermund. – 1992. XIII, 228 S. ISBN 3-515-06118-5

150 *Pakistan* / Zweite Heidelberger Südasiengespräche. Hrsg. von Dieter Conrad und Wolfgang-Peter Zingel. 1992. – IX, 162 S. ISBN 3-515-06168-1

151 Das brahmanische Totenritual nach der Antyeṣṭipaddhati des Nārāyaṇabhaṭṭa / von *Klaus-Werner Müller.* – 1992. XIII, 238 S. ISBN 3-515-06227-0

152 Verfassung und politische Kultur im Wandel : der indische Fürstenstaat Hyderabad 1911 - 48 / von *Margrit Pernau-Reifeld.* – 1992. VII, 424 S. ISBN 3-515-06231-9

153 Śaṃkara - mandāra - saurabha : eine Legende über das Leben des Philosophen Śaṃkara / [Nīlakaṇṭha]. Text, Übersetzung, Einleitung von *Anton Ungemach.* – 1992. IX, 187 S. ISBN 3-515-06232-7

154 Traditionelle Medizin auf den Philippinen : Angstbewältigung und Kognition bei Krankheiten / von *Norbert Kohnen.* – 1992. 396 S., Illus., graph. Darst. ISBN 3-515-05402-2

155 Das Puṣkara-Māhātmya : ein religionswissenschaftlicher Beitrag zum Wallfahrtsbegriff in Indien ; Erörterung, Text, Übersetzung / von *Aditya Malik.* – 1993. XIII, 408 S., Illus., Kt. ISBN 3-515-06358-7

156 Little kingdoms in Kalinga : Ideologie, Legitimation und Politik regionaler Eliten / von *Georg Berkemer.* – 1993. X, 396 S., Kt. ISBN 3-515-06444-3

157 The Tamil Tigers : armed struggle for identity / by *Dagmar Hellmann-Rajanayagam.* – 1994. X, 164 p. ISBN 3-515-06530-X

158 *Bangladesh* / Dritte Heidelberger Südasiengespräche. Hrsg. von Dieter Conrad und Wolfgang-Peter Zingel. – 1994. ISBN 3-515-06549-0

159 Grammatik des Alttamil : unter besonderer Berücksichtigung der Caṅkam-Texte des Dichters Kapilar / von *Thomas Lehmann.* – (in press)